Leisure Experience and
Human Development

D0732698

DATE DUE

LIVES IN CONTEXT
Mihaly Csikszentmihalyi

Leisure Experience and Human Development

A Dialectical Interpretation

DOUGLAS A. KLEIBER

University of Georgia

BASIC
BOOKS

A Member of the Perseus Books Group

Lives in Context

Copyright © 1999 by Basic Books, a Member of the Perseus Books Group

Published in 1999 in the United States of America by Basic Books, 10 East 53rd Street, New York, NY 10022

Library of Congress Cataloging-in-Publication Data
Kleiber, Douglas A.
  Leisure experience and human development : a dialectical
interpretation / Douglas A. Kleiber.
    p.   cm. — (Lives in context)
  Includes bibliographical references and index.
  ISBN 0-8133-3148-X (hardcover). — ISBN 0-8133-3149-8
(pbk.)
    1. Developmental psychology.   2. Leisure—Psychological aspects.
3. Play—Psychological aspects.   4. Self-actualization (Psychology).
I. Title.   II. Series.
BF713.K54   1999
790'.01'32—dc21   98-43804
                                                                        CIP

The paper used in this publication meets the requirements of the American National Standard for Permanence of Paper for Printed Library Materials Z39.48-1984.

10   9   8   7   6   5   4   3   2   1

To my parents

Contents

Tables and Figures

Tables

Figures

Preface

Leisure isn't what it used to be—for me or anyone else.

The interpretation given to it by Plato and Aristotle—an ideal state of being devoted primarily to contemplation, discourse, and self-expression—has been largely replaced with a more utilitarian version. The industrial revolution and the modern era have juxtaposed it with work and redefined it in terms of recovery and consumption. For the ancient Greeks, leisure needed no such justification.

I think I had something of that "unjustified" leisure as a child. My best recollection of it is in the image of seemingly endless summer evenings as a nine-year-old, creating a "dice baseball league" on the front porch. As a middle-aged man with limited free time, few play-mates, ailing joints, and a barrage of media-generated possibilities, it is something else again for me. What the future holds I glimpse in my parents and others who have aged more or less successfully, but the world will be a different place if and when I reach that age, and leisure will likely have changed as well.

This book is my attempt to examine the intersection of two fields of study: leisure studies and developmental psychology. I've kept a foot in both fields, being trained in the latter and having spent most of my academic life in the former. While straddling the fence has created its own challenges, it has also afforded me the advantage of an outsider's perspective, with some detachment from the agendas of each field.

At the University of Texas in 1969, I started my doctoral program in educational and developmental psychology while also serving as an assistant coach for the freshman football team. But as the tumultuous sixties were drawing to a close, I began to question the conventionality of sport and the impact it has on those who give it so much time and attention. Opportunities to do research on play and expressive behavior in childhood and adolescence captured my interest, and I cast an increasingly critical eye on the forces that undermine intrinsic motivation and self-expression, whether in classrooms or on playgrounds.

This perspective deepened with my first faculty position, teaching developmental psychology and learning theory in a teacher-preparation program. I came to realize that classroom environments are limited in their capacity to facilitate personal expressiveness. I was therefore attracted by an opportunity to move to a position in leisure studies at the University of Illinois, where I was able to focus my research and teaching on the context of leisure. As reluctant as I was to sever formal ties with the discipline of psychology, the position offered more time for research, and I was actually able to expand my study of human development while broadening my understanding of leisure-related phenomena.

As a formal academic pursuit, leisure studies in the late seventies was still a young field and welcomed the infusion of researchers from a variety of disciplines. Yet I was destined to remain something of an outsider in a field whose chief raison d'etre—then and now—is preparing undergraduates to work in leisure services, a field in which I had no professional experience. In many ways, though, the fit was better. Fortified by the conviction that play and self-expression had important developmental benefits, I was delighted that many of my new colleagues were public-spirited individuals who sought to enhance such activities, especially for those who were disadvantaged in some way.

The provision of services and resources is not *inevitably* advantageous to the well-being of individuals and communities, of course, and when the premise is accepted rather uncritically—as was too often the case in the field at that time—it can be a dangerous thing. Diversionary activities ("bread and circuses") have been used throughout history to divert attention from serious social problems and undermine attempts to improve living conditions. And even if government agencies were not interested in or capable of such diabolical control in the seventies, demand for evidence of the value of such services was also lacking.

The picture has changed considerably in recent years. Accountability demands in the public sector and the influx of social scientists has raised the profile of research and evaluation in recreation and leisure studies. Managers of leisure services are now moved to demonstrate the social, psychological, and economic "benefits" of their planning and programming. Moreover, the mission has been defined more clearly. Empowerment and development are now watchwords in the field, particularly with programs intended to remediate disabilities or disadvantages. This more visible commitment to responsibility for outcomes does not ensure their realization; but its compatibility with a critical perspective and with scientific evaluation has assuaged any regret I had about leaving psychology and education for the uncharted territory of leisure studies and recreation.

Still, I have several reservations about what is now my field. First, there is insufficient attention in recreation and leisure studies to the relationship between expressive activity and development (though the same may be said of psychology as well). While I address the issue more closely in Chapters 4 and 5, the impact of activity involvement on psychological and social development has not received significant research attention. In those rare cases where it has been assessed, the evidence is mixed at best—for example, sport is *not* a builder of character except in very specific circumstances.

Second, the activity bias in recreation is unself-consciously consistent with the "busy-ness" that is the dis-ease of contemporary life. If the leisure of childhood ever persisted into adolescence and adulthood, it rarely does now. Instead, we have "hurry sickness," which threatens the health of many who are swept along by the rapids of everyday life. The field of leisure services has yet to seriously address the extent to which peacefulness can enhance adjustment and reflection can promote development.

The third reservation I have about the field of leisure studies is that individual differences are often neglected, especially in practice. Age, gender, ethnicity, and socioeconomic status can determine when and where leisure is a problem and when and how it can offer a solution. The conventional claims for a consistently positive influence of recreation on well-being fail to consider exactly who the intended beneficiaries might be and in what ways the activity might work for some but not for others.

Finally, though, there is a certain incongruity in *providing* for leisure. Those who have studied leisure commonly associate it with the freedom to do what you want when you want. Formal recreation, with prearranged programs structured by others, can at times be as confining as school and work. Of course, those who participate in structured programs do so voluntarily and expect intrinsic satisfaction. And structure, as I will argue, can foster the most rewarding leisure and recreation. But relying on others to provide leisure opportunities is inherently limiting to self-expression.

In analyzing the relationship between leisure experience and human development, I will treat development as both a *process* of change and as a *sequence* of predictable, age-related changes. While confining my analysis to the contemporary Western world, I will attempt to show (1) how leisure is predictably influenced by age-related changes in contemporary life and (2) how experiences common to leisure can facilitate personal growth. At the same time, however, I will consider relevant individual differences, especially gender, and historical and social contexts as well.

Among the developmental questions that guide this work, then, are the following: what changes in a person, what endures, and why? If, as some postmodernists have asserted, there are no predictable patterns, if the "self" and "meaning" are mere constructs assembled from the pastiche of possibilities suggested in the media and social life, then such questions become meaningless. In a sense, if the postmodernists are right, then developmentalists are out of work. But my view is that there are still predictable patterns of behavior change over the human life span that tell us about development. And to the extent that we are in an age where structural determinants of behavior and personality such as religion, occupation, nationality, and regional identification have lost much of their determining hold, leisure becomes especially relevant to development as it is individually constructed; if people are in a position to invent themselves, it will occur most readily within the freedom that is available.

Some of the chapters that follow deal with specific groups—adolescents, people with disabilities, the aged—but the aim here is to speak more to the general patterns in which self-expression and enjoyment emerge during a person's life, how freedom and opportunity are constructed and used along the way, and what impact leisure has on stability and change in individuals. This general problem should be of interest to those with backgrounds in both developmental psychology and leisure studies who want to understand expressive behavior and the ways in which time, freedom, and enjoyment are and can be used developmentally.

Nevertheless, some readers might want to spend more time with the first chapter on the meaning of leisure, while for others the excursion into developmental issues in Chapter 2 may be of more interest. Chapter 3 treats leisure as a consequence of development and addresses the changes in expressive behavior that occur across the life span. Chapters 4 and 5 turn the tables and consider the impact of leisure on both socialization and identity formation, while Chapter 6 discusses leisure as a resource for adjusting to and transcending negative life events.

Chapters 7 and 8 then bring the book to a close by examining the significance of leisure for middle age and later life.

As with any book, this one reflects the influence and assistance of many people. I am indebted to Mike Csikszentmihalyi in particular for his invitation to do this book, for his encouragement along the way, and most of all for the continuing inspiration of his ideas. At once esteemed colleagues, trusted friends, and thoughtful critics, Reed Larson, Seppo Iso-Ahola, Roger Mannell, and Brian Sutton-Smith have influenced this effort in both their published words and their thoughtful guidance and encouragement.

After Lynn Morris reviewed the initial proposal, Linda Caldwell and Val Freysinger took on the task of reviewing the first complete draft. If I have failed to do justice to their good suggestions, it is through no fault of theirs. And their support of the project is deeply appreciated, as is that of Cathy Murphy and others at Westview Press.

Students at the University of Georgia and the University of Manitoba also played significant roles as auditors for the early versions of some of the chapters that follow. Their confusion about some of my preliminary thoughts has been as useful as their clearly framed challenges in helping me identify what needed to be changed. Doctoral students at UGA provided assistance, both paid and unpaid, that went well beyond the call of duty. Susan Hutchinson gave most of an assistantship to this project in tracking down sources and reviewing multiple drafts, creating a dialog with the material along the way. Richard Williams, Nancy Jekubovich, Diane Groff, and Gary Green also provided critical readings of parts of the book, as did Don Greer from the University of Nebraska, Omaha, and Cheryl Baldwin from the University of Iowa.

Finally, my family—Pam and Molly and Ryan—have done what families often do when a member is preoccupied with an overwhelming project: they supported the effort lovingly and faithfully in whatever ways they could. But Pam went well beyond that in critically reviewing every draft and in being a true friend and companion when the writing became lonely and difficult. It was a labor of love for both of us.

Douglas A. Kleiber
Athens, Georgia

1 The Many Faces of Leisure

The subject of leisure has challenged writers and scholars throughout recorded history.[1] The ancient Greeks regarded it as an ideal human condition, *schole,* that reflected freedom from obligation and attention to the refinement of character. Cultivation of one's intellect and talents, and social discourse about public affairs were celebrated as its highest forms.

History has significantly changed both the context and meaning of leisure, giving rise to a multiplicity of concepts and practices. Occasional efforts to resurrect the Greek ideal notwithstanding,[2] the notions that leisure is essentially discretionary time or, alternatively, that it is a collection of enjoyable past times have prevailed. Most people think of it as the time-space that remains after work and other obligations have been discharged and/or as the sum of activities for which this time-space is used.

Even for those in the field of leisure studies, for whom leisure has professional as well as academic significance, the term has eluded consensus. Research has confirmed the popular association of leisure with the following elements, in varying combinations: free time, expressive activities, special occasions, relaxation, and enjoyment.[3] Researchers often equate leisure with free time for a pragmatic reason: it is relatively easy to assess, being easily distinguishable from time devoted to meeting contractual obligations or maintaining one's physical welfare. But this equation has been criticized for defining leisure only negatively, in terms of what it is *not,* and thus failing to identify what it *is.* Having time at one's disposal does not ensure a particular state of mind or even a sense of freedom. One's *apparent* freedom may be clouded by feelings of regret, anxiety, apprehension, remorse, guilt, duty, or depression, hardly the ingredients in anyone's recipe for leisure. What, then, *is* the contemporary experience of leisure?

One attractive answer is to equate leisure with enjoyment and see in "pure" or "true" leisure, or "the leisure state," the qualities associated with deep involvement.[4] This deep involvement has been compared with *flow,* the creative absorption described by rock climbers, painters, dancers, surgeons, and others interviewed by Mihaly Csikszentmihalyi.[5] More will be said about this experience later, but it is often used in research to approximate *the* leisure experience, as if there is only one.

The connection between leisure and flow has been studied experimentally as well. Roger Mannell tested the assumption that enjoyable activity brings about intense absorption that leads predictably to the misperception of the passage of time and a lack of attention to one's surroundings,[6] characteristics associated with flow experience. In his studies subjects were provided varying degrees of choice with respect to what were predicted to be absorbing activities (e.g., playing board games). After a period of involvement, the subjects were asked how much they remembered about the room and how much time they thought had gone by. Those who had more choice in the matter and who indicated that they enjoyed the activity more showed signs of more intense absorption; they thought time had gone by faster than others did and than it actually had, and they remembered less about their surroundings. The fact that exposure to gamelike activities in conditions of choice resulted in flowlike involvement lends some support to the contention that leisure can be characterized experientially and further that it can be manipulated experimentally.

Still, the contrivance associated with experimental manipulation seems almost antithetical to leisure. We are not accustomed to using the word *leisure* to characterize such constrained circumstances, however much we end up liking the activity. More accurately, this research suggests that intense absorption or enjoyment has the power to transform task-oriented, structured situations into something that *seems* more like leisure than work. When people say offhandedly that "my work is my leisure," their point is usually that they enjoy their work rather than that they would literally call it leisure. In fact, there is evidence that flow experience is more common in work than in free time.[7] So, if flowlike enjoyment doesn't distinguish leisure from other contexts, what does?

Research on the connotative meaning of leisure,[8] or what people think of when asked about the feelings they associate with it, has revealed that leisure suggests some combination of the perception of freedom of choice, intrinsic motivation, freedom from evaluation, relaxation, and enjoyment. The first three define the context of leisure, its preconditions rather than its characteristics. Enjoyment and relaxation, on the other hand, reflect what might be regarded as common, prototypical leisure experiences. But consider their differences. Reminiscing with a friend while sitting in rocking chairs on the front porch and hang gliding over the California coast don't seem to fit in the same category—indeed, they might be viewed as occupying opposite ends on a continuum of activation. What, then, if anything, binds them together as leisure? To be sure, both are freely chosen and intrinsically rewarding. But their differences lead to the conclusion that these are distinct experiences that fall under the umbrella of leisure and cannot, therefore, define it.

Leisure as Context

For our purposes, let us regard leisure as *the combination of free time and the expectation of preferred experience.* Thus leisure extends freedom beyond discretion, lack of obligation, or the vacuity of simple nonwork time and includes the absence of worry and a sense of opportunity and possibility. We recognize the context of leisure when time is really felt as free, when it is distinguishable from that devoted to obligation or necessity and evokes a sense of opportunity.

The relativity of the freedom in free time is also important to recognize. Conditions of constraint, demand, and responsibility vary dramatically in their impact on leisure. In some situations—in war, an abusive relationship, abject poverty, or extended caregiving, for example—leisure is either impossible or unwanted.[9] But where circumstances afford some diminution of external demands or the opportunity for disengagement from elective commitments, leisure is often experienced as a *change* in perspective. It is a new setting, a new stage of operations. It is marked off, or framed, in some way as something different from what preceded it and as being ultimately limited by a need to return to what will follow. So, for example, a parent of a five-year-old and a two-year-old experiences leisure *with* the five-year-old when the two-year-old takes a nap and, at another time, with a friend whom she joins for a walk when the babysitter arrives.

Preferred experiences are those sought from activities directly and immediately; they are not those that follow from instrumental and otherwise unappealing activities. In other words, they are intrinsically rather than extrinsically motivated. Leisure contrasts most dramatically with work when the work is done only in exchange for some external reward or payoff. When the work is a preferred, intrinsically motivated experience, a "labor of love," it is likely to be classifiable as leisure, providing that it is distinguishable from other more urgent activities of daily living. The enthusiastic gardener offers an apt example. The growth of the plants gives the activity meaning and justification, but the activity is embraced primarily as a respite from other activities.

Seeing leisure simply as the *envelope* containing the variety of experiences that occur during free time allows us to define things more clearly for purposes of both research and practice. But there is more to say about the feeling of leisure per se, about the emotion that is experienced when leisure is recognized as being at hand. Recall the point that discretionary time may be beset with emotional difficulties and may even be a burden to those without the resources to act effectively. In contrast, the experience of freedom that one feels at the onset of a leisure episode—whether pausing to rock on the porch or putting the hang-gliding equipment in the van—persists over the duration of the activity and is recognized, at least in retrospect, as an *opportunity* for gratifying experience.

There is a sense of freedom that comes from disengaging from the activities required by work, school, and family life; and exercising freedom *from* other demands often affords the freedom *to* act in particular ways. And engagement in activities in which attention is fully invested perpetuates a sense of disengagement from ordinary life.[10] In that sense, the transcendence felt in the reverie of the porch rocker differs only in degree and intensity from that of a hang glider poised at the edge of a steep cliff.

Producing leisure by disengaging from other areas of life may be more characteristic of males than females in most cultures, however. For females consistently involved in nurturing others, the argument goes, such disengagement is neither as possible nor as necessary for enjoyment or relaxation. In Western cultures leisure for mothers and grandmothers has typically been somewhat more fluid in integrating and accommodating role responsibilities than is the case for their male counterparts.[11] While a picnic may be a leisure outing for the whole family, for a mother it is also another meal to prepare. Nevertheless, in one study women were as likely as men to identify *separateness* as central to memorable leisure experiences.[12] Furthermore, both men and women often find a way to attend to home and family in the context of leisure. Whether it is created by a distinct change in focus or incorporated into role responsibilities along the way, it is the freedom of expression that engenders a sense of leisure. In contrast, under conditions of poverty, hunger, or fear of crime or abuse, leisure is impossible regardless of role relations.

If leisure is constructed around a sense of freedom, however, what should we make of those free-time activities that require a commitment to a schedule or that cause stress or discomfort? Freedom and enjoyment might be threatened under these conditions. Being a group member of an organization usually entails scheduled meetings and some role responsibilities. And even many activities and vacations that are freely and enthusiastically initiated meet with difficulties and frustration. Does leisure end at the point at which a person has a flat tire on the road to a national park or when the horse is pulling stubbornly against the rider's reins? Or what about the feeling of not wanting to attend yet another meeting despite being one of the group's initial organizers? The experience obviously changes at such points. In some sense, the "spell" of leisure—at least that associated with an easy, relaxed attitude of mind—is broken. Yet, however tenuous its hold at times, leisure accommodates a wide range of experiences.

Manifestations of Preferred Experience

If leisure is a context of relative freedom that presents opportunities for preferred experience, it may include a variety of experiences ranging from *intense involvement* to *relaxed detachment*. Among the more common of these is *fun*. *Fun* is a word that, like enjoyment and leisure, may be extended to include a variety of circumstances, but the word usually has a social connotation often associated with smiling and laughter.[13] Again, fun does not define leisure but rather, like relaxation and intense involvement, commonly falls within its realm. These experiences can differ so much that they are marked by overtly distinguishable facial expressions. Imagine the smiling face of someone bantering with a friend, the serious expression of someone working with clay on a potter's wheel, and the somewhat blank and passive expression of someone watching a talk show on television. The idea that some emotions are expressed facially has received considerable support in psychological research,[14] but the notion is used here just to highlight the contrast in experiences.

A fourth experience, *excitement*, is also worth recognizing as distinguishable in most instances from the other three. Whether it results from reading a murder mystery, riding a raft down a raging river, or watching the conclusion of a tightly contested soccer match, the notion of excitement may more accurately capture the emotional tenor of a particular leisure occasion than the other three experiences described. Excitement may share the intensity, the deep involvement, and the focused attention of a flow experience; but where flow requires moderate levels of arousal for optimal control and performance, excitement takes arousal higher.

Let these diverse experiences constitute the experiential parameters for this discussion, then. But they by no means exhaust the subjective conditions that are sought and felt in leisure: consider the tears that come with sad movies and books, for example. Rather, they represent the more commonly sought experiences of leisure, in my view, and the wide range of emotions to be found therein. Nor are they mutually exclusive. In fact, a leisure occasion may include all or any combination of them.

Let us continue, though, by examining the two experiences, intense involvement and relaxation, that are the most likely to be developmentally useful, albeit in different ways.

Taking Leisure Seriously

In Robert Stebbins's work on *serious leisure*,[15] weekend musicians, mushroom collectors, amateur astronomers, and barbershop singers, among others, described their activities as being intensely enjoyable and involving. However, they also revealed that pain, discomfort, and personal sacrifice are common to these activities and that commitment to the group often entailed worklike requirements such as practice, scheduling, and time management. As leisure activities become more important to an individual, inconveniences such as flat tires and social constraints such as membership dues and meetings often become acceptable parts of the whole. Creating such a sense of commitment and obligation can even enhance the experience of enjoyment. This happens in two ways: (1) the commitments reflected in belonging to an organization or being a member of a family can structure experience as something special, around which life can be organized;[16] and (2) if something is risked or *staked* in an activity, the participant's absorption is often deepened.[17] Taking lessons or buying equipment is the kind of stake that Howard Becker referred to as a "side bet";[18] it raises the level of commitment and thereby increases the intensity of involvement and often the level of performance as well. Notwithstanding obligation and commitment, the action is still acknowledged as voluntary and discretionary.

To illustrate the idea of a stake, consider the game of basketball. One can shoot baskets in the driveway, but there is a great deal more at stake in an organized basketball game with spectators and with league standings hinging on the outcome. Or compare harmonizing with a group of friends on the street corner with performing at a festival in front of hundreds of people. Such conditions can be as sobering as hang-gliding when casual spontaneity and playfulness are sacrificed in the interest of focusing attention to achieve first-rate performance. That such intensity may still fit within the context of leisure is supported by the fact that the activities are selected with this experience in mind.[19]

Leisure researchers have referred to such activities as high-involvement or high-investment activities[20] and have recognized their importance to personal identity and quality of life. Similarly, studies of *enduring involvement* in leisure have focused on the importance and symbolic value of activities such as camping and fishing, using survey items such as "When I am [doing X], others see me the way I want them to see me" and "I find that a lot of my life is organized around [X]."[21]

The second way in which commitment can facilitate the experience of leisure and enjoyment is in structuring experience. This is also paradoxical because responding to a set of requirements entails relinquishing choice, and freedom of choice is commonly associated with leisure. But freedom should not be equated with choice; nor is it always a reflection of control.

The absence of choice can certainly compromise a sense of freedom, but it does not follow that a bounty of choices enhances that experience. Social psychologists have determined that beyond an optimal number, choices are experienced as burdensome to decision makers—consider the experience of navigating the aisles of a huge supermarket, for example.[22] Or more to the subject of leisure, consider the information overload that many feel in choosing among television channels or Web sites. In fact, making the decision is what feels liberating in such cases.

According to William Harper, the opportunity for "ongoing consent" in a decision makes choice largely irrelevant to the meaning of freedom in leisure.[23] Freedom is "undergone," in Harper's view, as one is drawn into an activity and acts in accordance with it. This kind of surrendering to the activity relinquishes choice in the interest of full commitment. Studies of recreation trips support this idea. The consideration of various choices and options is associated with relatively low mood states, whereas enthusiasm rises once the decision has been made.[24]

Such surrender occurs most readily in immediately compelling activities such as white-water rafting. But it may also result from other commitments, such as caring for one's grandchildren. A sense of obligation in such activities might seem to render the motivation extrinsic rather than intrinsic, but making a commitment can put one in a better position to relax and surrender to whatever happens.

Relaxation: How Well Do We Pause?

The idea of surrendering suggests a degree of trust, faith, and, indeed, comfort with one's surroundings. Oftentimes, to have leisure is simply to relax. This is the essential view of Josef Pieper, who argues that relinquishing the mundane affairs of everyday reality, at least temporarily, and attaining peace allows one to give fuller attention to spiritual matters. Such devotion does not require effort, in Pieper's view, but is instead the result of relaxed openness and appreciation of the gift of life.[25] For Pieper, leisure is first of all an attitude of mind that celebrates and affirms one's humanness—a receptive and effortless condition of the soul.

While Pieper's view may be inconsistent with contemporary conceptions of leisure, his view is echoed in everyday language, which bespeaks the contrast between leisure and effort. Dictionary definitions tell us that to do something "leisurely" is to do it "casually" or "in an easy, relaxed manner" that implies an abundance of time. Similarly, when someone suggests that you respond "at your leisure," it is an invitation to respond in a relaxed, unhurried manner, when time and occasion allow.

More generally, though, relaxing means disengaging from action; it is a treasured, even necessary, compensation for a rushed and demanding existence. But it can offer more than just emotional adjustment. Leisure as relaxation is likely to involve temporal reflection, a pausing to gain perspective, to register appreciation, and simply to experience the here and now.

In *Freedom and Destiny* the psychoanalyst Rollo May discusses the significance of *the pause* as a critical element of freedom and creativity.[26] The pause, a notion more at home in Eastern than Western thought, signifies what is *not* rather than what is. The pause signifies appreciation and opportunity; it is time pregnant with possibility. But it also represents a kind of resistance, an interruption of "the rigid chain of cause and effect":

> In the person's life response no longer blindly follows stimulus. There intervenes between the two our human imaginings, reflections, considerations, ponderings. Pause is the prerequisite for wonder. When we don't pause, when we are perpetually hurrying from one appointment to another, from one "planned activity" to another, we sacrifice the richness of wonder.[27]

May notes that musicians are especially aware of the power of pauses in giving notes meaning and clarity. He links the pause to creativity more directly in seeing it as "inviting the Muses," the process whereby painters, poets, and other artists put themselves in a position of "readiness for the 'lucky accident.'"[28] The pause takes advantage of the capacity to appreciate. In everyday thought reflection requires pausing; and yet pauses can last as long as a weekend, a vacation, or a sabbatical. But May also notes that the American sense of leisure does not make particularly good use of the pause—in contrast to that of European and non-Western cultures—preferring to define the freedom of leisure in its potential for action, in movement and becoming rather than in contemplation and being. This active tilt might explain why the work of Josef Pieper, which sees in leisure a receptive rather than an active state, has received so little attention in American leisure studies. May suggests that the letting be or letting happen that one does in wandering an unfamiliar city or "wasting time" in some other way "may turn out to be the most significant thing one can do."[29] The significance comes in the reflection it affords for making meaning and charting direction. As with serious leisure, then, we see in relaxed leisure the potential for influencing developmental processes.

The Place of Leisure in the Study of Development

Until recently the subject of leisure has had a very minor place in discussions of human development. To be sure, the embracing of a life-span perspective has given leisure some significance in the study of retirement and aging. And play—a forerunner of adolescent and adult leisure—has been a regular subject for research on child development. But attention to leisure behavior in the years between childhood and old age has been largely absent.

There are at least two explanations for this. First, there is the question of meaning. The differences in meaning just reviewed have not been conducive to clearly defining leisure. Having argued that activity and experiential definitions are too limiting to capture all that is understood as leisure, let me return to the following: leisure is *the context of free time in combination with the expectation of preferred experience.*

The second explanation for the limited treatment of leisure behavior in studies of human development is the assumption that such behavior is psychologically unimportant.[30] If viewed merely as entertainment, leisure is of limited relevance to the more serious requirements of living. Indeed, the quest for diversion might well be regarded as immature and dismissed as regressive except for the awareness of a need to adjust to and compensate for such requirements. If the vicissitudes of work, homemaking, and war generate the need for occasional rest and relaxation, those discretionary diversions are rarely seen as very important in themselves. But triviality is not the only alternative to urgency and necessity; there are activities for which the yardstick of importance is not external compulsion but internal need, activities in which the quest for meaning and value is an end in itself rather than the means to an imposed end. As one writer put it, "What makes an activity desirable and not merely desired is that an individual would want to engage in that activity if he were thinking clearly and were fully informed."[31]

In reality, though, leisure rarely reaches its potential for promoting self-directed development. Instead, as with other forms of human capital, it is vastly underutilized and misappropriated. Too often free time is wasted time: energy dissipated without creativity or even restorative value, and in many cases with socially and personally destructive results. What, then, are the conditions of leisure that make it valuable for human development? This is the question we will address in the chapters to come.

Plan of This Book

The next chapter addresses development as it follows both chronologically with age and as a response to a person's intrinsically motivated inclinations. Leisure contexts, with minimal external influences, afford a wide variety of opportunities for exploration of possibilities, expression of interests, and experimentation with action alternatives.

Chapter 3 shows leisure largely as a reflection or product of development, tracing changes in leisure behavior and experience over the life course. It also attempts to disentangle the changes that are inevitable from those that are merely tied to a particular culture (primarily North American) as we approach the turn of the century. The chapter also examines leisure patterns that are accepted aspects of contemporary culture even though they are developmentally useless or even destructive.

The five chapters that follow address five problems or themes that I have come to regard as important in both the study of leisure and the study of development: socialization, identity formation, transcending negative life events, the dialectics of middle age, and personal integration in later life. This organization represents a linear progression across the life span. Since each chapter has a very different focus, the reader will not find an age-graded, inclusive study of each problem across the entire life course. Nevertheless, these chapters are intended to have a "reach," both forward and backward in the life span.[32]

Chapter 4 focuses on play and leisure as socializing influences in early and middle childhood. The emphasis in this chapter is on personal and social integration, with attention to emotional, moral, and social development and the shaping of competence and achievement orientations. But the stresses associated with overaccommodation are also considered. Overstructuring "free time" activities is common where fear of crime and delinquency is pervasive or where such activities are seen as conducive to social integration and social mobility despite the costs to experimentalism, innovation, and creativity.

With Chapter 5 the emphasis is on differentiating tendencies as the focus turns to the way exploration and personal expressiveness in leisure experience contribute to identity formation. Here again, though, I examine the destabilizing impact of excessive and continuing differentiation in play and leisure in the absence of personal and social integration.

Chapter 6 departs from the emphasis on the individual-society dialectic and turns instead to the problem of adjustment to some of the significant events that people face and the role and place of leisure in response to those events. Some events, such as graduation and retirement, are predictable, whereas others, such as a paralyzing injury or the loss of one's home in a fire, are not. Adulthood is the general age frame here because part of the impact of such events comes in the realization of the impermanence of being "all grown-up" and understanding that change is inevitable. Whether such change results in positive adaptations and even progressive development or degeneration and despair is the principal issue. Leisure may be less important in creating change in such circumstances than in allowing one to adjust to and cope with the changes that occur. Leisure experience may thus serve as a *buffer,* providing some continuity and stability in the face of change.

Chapter 7 returns to a theme of the earlier chapters in addressing the subject of social accommodation. The task of *individuation,* which Daniel Levinson associates with midlife, recreates issues of autonomy that are characteristic of earlier ages.[33] On the other hand, Erik Erikson argues that isolation and stagnation are the costs of becoming too self-possessed.[34] Leisure is, of course, implicated in patterns of self-absorption and self-indulgence; but some of this may be a necessary antidote to the excessive accommodation that characterized the preceding "establishment" years. Thus, Chapter 7 addresses the ways in which midlife leisure facilitates renewal and self-invention on the one hand and generativity on the other.

Chapter 8 examines the subject of aging, where leisure often gains preeminence, at least in principle. An abundance of free time can be particularly problematic for cohorts who have been committed to the value of work and self-sacrifice all of their lives. Being and staying engaged is seen as the best, and in some cases the only, antidote to idleness and self-indulgence. Furthermore, the prospect of deterioration and despair associated with inactivity makes retreat from action and involvement ill advised. But disengagement from some involvement becomes necessary as physical and social limitations require some degree of repose. Here again, the individual-society dialectic creates an inevitable tension; the personal integration that Erikson and others call for in optimizing this concluding segment of life may require both interaction with and distance from others.[35]

The extent to which older people use leisure for personal integration through reminiscence suggests the importance of privacy, space, and solitude; it also points to the value of a generous and caring other. According to many gerontologists, meaning making is the key to establishing well-being and ego integrity in later life. But then meaning making may be what gives leisure importance throughout life.

Notes

1. S. deGrazia, *Of Time, Work and Leisure* (New York: Anchor, 1962); B. Dare, G. Welton, and W. Coe, *Leisure in Western Thought: A Critical and Historical Analysis* (Dubuque: Kendall/Hunt, 1987).

2. deGrazia, *Of Time, Work and Leisure.*

3. For example, B. Gunter, "The Leisure Experience: Selected Properties," *Journal of Leisure Research* 19 (1987): 115–130; W. Harper, "Freedom in the Experience of Leisure," *Leisure Sciences* 8 (1986): 115–130; D. M. Samdahl, "A Symbolic Interactionist Model of Leisure," *Leisure Sciences* 10 (1988): 27–39; S. Shaw, "The Meaning of Leisure in Everyday Life," *Leisure Sciences* 7 (1985): 1–24.

4. H. A. Tinsley and D. J. Tinsley, "A Theory of Attributes, Benefits, and Causes of Leisure Experience," *Leisure Sciences* 8 (1986): 1–45.

5. M. Csikszentmihalyi, *Beyond Boredom and Anxiety* (San Francisco: Jossey-Bass, 1975); *Flow: The Psychology of Optimal Experience* (New York: Harper & Row, 1990).

6. R. Mannell, "Social Psychological Techniques and Strategies for Studying Leisure Experiences," in S. Iso-Ahola, ed., *Social Psychological Perspectives on Leisure and Recreation* (Springfield, IL: C. C. Thomas, 1980); R. Mannell and W. Bradley, "Does Greater Freedom Always Lead to Greater Leisure? Testing a Person x Environment Model of Freedom and Leisure," *Journal of Leisure Research* 18 (1986): 215–230.

7. M. Csikszentmihalyi and J. Lefevre, "Optimal Experience in Work and Leisure," *Journal of Personality and Social Psychology* 36 (1989): 815–822.

8. S. E. Iso-Ahola, *The Social Psychology of Leisure and Recreation* (Dubuque: W. C. Brown, 1980); J. Neulinger, *The Psychology of Leisure* (Springfield, IL: C. C. Thomas, 1981); Shaw, "The Meaning of Leisure in Everyday Life."

9. See, for example, N. Weinblatt and L. Navon, "Flight from Leisure: A Neglected Phenomenon in Leisure Studies," *Leisure Sciences* 17 (1993):

309–325; R. V. Russell and S. K. Stage, "Leisure as Burden: Sudanese Refugee Women," *Journal of Leisure Research* 2 (1996): 108–121.

10. For more on this idea, see D. Kleiber, "Motivational Reorientation in Adulthood and the Resource of Leisure," in D. Kleiber and M. Maehr, eds., *Motivation and Adulthood* (Greenwich, CT: JAI Press, 1985).

11. L. Bella, "Beyond Androcentrism: Women and Leisure," in E. Jackson and T. Burton, eds., *Understanding Leisure and Recreation: Mapping the Past, Charting the Future* (State College, PA: Venture Publishing, 1989).

12. Gunter, "The Leisure Experience."

13. W. Podilchak, "Distinctions of Fun, Enjoyment and Leisure," *Leisure Studies* 10 (1991): 133–148; "Establishing Fun in Leisure," *Leisure Sciences* 13 (1991): 123–136.

14. P. Ekman and W. V. Friesen, *Unmasking the Face: A Guide to Recognizing Emotions from Facial Clues* (Englewood Cliffs, NJ: Prentice-Hall, 1975); J. Reeve, "The Face of Interest," *Motivation and Emotion* 17 (1993): 353–375.

15. R. Stebbins, *Amateurs, Professionals, and Serious Leisure* (Montreal: McGill-Queen's University Press, 1992).

16. R. Mannell, "High-investment Activity and Life Satisfaction Among Older Adults: Committed, Serious Leisure and Flow," in J. R. Kelly, ed., *Activity and Aging: Staying Involved in Later Life* (Newbury Park, CA: Sage, 1993), 125–144.

17. Csikszentmihalyi, *Beyond Boredom and Anxiety*; Mannell, "High-investment Activity"; Stebbins, *Amateurs*.

18. H. Becker, "Notes on the Concept of Commitment," *American Journal of Sociology* 66 (1960): 32–40.

19. B. Shamir, "Commitment and Leisure," *Sociological Perspectives* 31 (1988): 238–258.

20. See, for example, Mannell, "High-investment Activity"; J. R. Kelly, M. W. Steinkamp, and J. Kelly, "Later Life Satisfaction: Does Leisure Contribute?" *Leisure Sciences* 9 (1987): 189–200.

21. N. McIntyre, "The Personal Meaning of Participation: Enduring Involvement," *Journal of Leisure Research* 21 (1989): 167–179; see also M. Havitz and F. Dimanche, "Leisure Involvement Revisited. Conceptual Conundrums and Measurement Advances," *Journal of Leisure Research* 29 (1997): 245–278, for a review of this work.

22. I. D. Steiner. "Perceived Freedom," in B. Maher, ed., *Advances in Experimental Social Psychology*, vol. 5 (New York: Academic Press, 1970).

23. Harper, "Freedom in the Experience of Leisure."

24. W. Hammitt, "Outdoor Recreation: Is It a Multi-phase Experience?" *Journal of Leisure Research* 12 (1980): 107–115; J. L. Berger and R. Schreyer, *The Experiential Aspects of Recreation: A Review of Relevant Literature and*

Suggestions for Future Research (Unpublished report for the Department of Forest Resources. Logan, UT: Utah State University, 1986).

25. J. Pieper, *Leisure: The Basis of Culture* (New York: Pantheon, 1952).

26. R. May, *Freedom and Destiny* (New York: W. W. Norton, 1981).

27. Ibid., 167.

28. Ibid., 171.

29. Ibid., 177.

30. There is little argument that leisure is *economically* important, being second only to health care in total public/private expenditure in the United States.

31. W. E. Cooper, "Some Philosophical Aspects of Leisure Theory," in E. L. Jackson and T. L. Burton, eds., *Understanding Leisure and Recreation* (State College, PA: Venture Press, 1989), 54.

32. I use life span and life course interchangeably in this analysis. Life span tends to be preferred by psychologists and life course by sociologists; and while psychology is more central to my approach, I have benefitted from the perspectives of both disciplines.

33. D. Levinson, C. Darrow, F. Klein, M. Levinson, and B. McKee, *The Season's of a Man's Life* (New York: Alfred Knopf, 1978); D. Levinson (with J. Levinson), *The Seasons of a Woman's Life* (New York: Alfred Knopf, 1990).

34. E. Erikson, *Childhood and Society* (New York: Norton, 1963).

35. Dialectics of development have been discussed by a number of authors including Klaus Riegel, "The Dialectics of Human Development," *American Psychologist* 31 (1976): 689–700, and Allan R. Buss, *A Dialectical Psychology* (New York: Wiley, 1979). The approach has also been applied to the study of leisure by J. R. Kelly in *Leisure Identities and Interactions* (London: Allen & Unwin, 1983) and *Freedom to Be* (New York: Macmillan, 1987) from a sociological perspective, and by Seppo Iso-Ahola in *The Social Psychology of Leisure and Recreation,* and Valeria Freysinger in "The Dialectics of Leisure and Development for Women and Men at Midlife," *Journal of Leisure Research* 27 (1995): 61–84.

2 Development, Motivation, and Leisure

The central argument of this book is that leisure offers conditions for optimizing human development and self-actualization. This position is based on two premises: (1) that leisure is a context of relative freedom for self-expression and (2) that development can be at least partially self-directed. In the following pages we will examine both of these premises as well as the mediating role of motivation in the leisure and development relationship.

The study of development has traditionally been mostly about age-related change. In that sense, leisure behavior and experience are merely expressions of the dynamic biological and social forces that bring about such change. In the language of science, development (age-related change) is the independent variable, and leisure behavior the dependent variable. Nevertheless, more recent studies of the forces that bring about development, whether age-related or not, have accorded increased recognition to individual initiatives that interact with the environment. Contemporary "action" theories of development rely on this notion of initiative.[1]

Shifting views of human development arise in part from changes in the social sciences more generally. Poststructuralist/postmodernist thought asserts that the considerable weakening of traditional behavioral influences—culture, race, family, religion, nationality, and region—has given people the leeway to reinvent themselves, although the influences of media and marketing have rendered this autonomy somewhat illusory. My view, which is shared by many contemporary developmentalists, is that the truth lies somewhere in between for most people: notwithstanding the undeniable power of social influences, people retain the potential for self-determination. This chapter deals with the changing views of development that have given motivation and leisure more important roles to play.

Sources of Development

Development connotes permanent, irreversible systemic change. To the extent that it is biologically driven, as it is in childhood more than in adulthood, we can often associate an age with it—for example, the contrarian "terrible twos" and the onset of abstract thought in the transition to adolescence. But whether the result of biological maturation, experience, or both, development is directed largely by two processes: *differentiation* and *hierarchical integration*.[2] Differentiation is the diversification that leads one to be other than what one was before; integration is the force that reconnects a differentiated part to the whole and that reorganizes the individual at a more complex and sophisticated level.

In the interaction of differentiation and integration, which Heinz Werner referred to as the *orthogenetic principle*, an organism becomes less stimulus-bound and less impelled by its own emotional state. For humans, this means that the growing child becomes better able to use freedom and opportunity for his or her own purposes. Differentiation and hierarchical integration are adaptive life forces that have a strong biological imperative; but they are triggered not only by experience but also by freedom and self-direction.

Past developmental models have differed primarily in the relative weight accorded to organic/biological and environmental influences on behavior and behavioral change. The "nature versus nurture" debate, usually ending with some recognition that nature and nurture interact to create their effects in most cases, has rarely entertained the idea that individuals might actually exercise some control over both influences.

The prevalence of social and biological determinism in models of development has not made much room in the past for self-direction. Humanistic psychology has always given developmentalists reasons to consider the importance of intrinsically motivated self-expression and creativity; but only recently have developmental psychology circles recognized individuals as agents in their *own* development.

This is not to suggest, of course, that such self-direction operates independently of social forces. Indeed, the environment impinges on behavior in a wide variety of ways. Ecological perspectives on devel-

opment describe the confluence of many factors: home, neighborhood, school, the political climate of a community, and all their interactions.[3] Self-determination is invariably conditioned by these myr-
iad social influences. Some exigent social circumstances—poverty and
oppression, for example—circumscribe individual initiative more
than others, but age-related demands and expectations can also be so
compelling that they give developmental "stage" models the look of
inevitability. The needs for autonomy and sexual intimacy that lead a
young man to leave home, for example, are reinforced by normative
social pressures.

Developmental Stages and Tasks

Researchers and parents alike have embraced the idea of developmental stages. When particular ways of thinking and behaving can be associated with certain ages, it becomes much easier to document and
manage developmental change. Knowing what to expect at a given
age has practical and theoretical advantages. As noted earlier, the pre-
diction game becomes considerably more difficult after childhood,
but there are models of development and aging that continue to have
validity and applicability, even as history marches through the postmodern era. Chief among these is that of Erik Erikson,[4] which, while
based initially on the psychosexual stages of childhood outlined by
Sigmund Freud, was continually expanded to include historical and
social as well as biological/organismic influences over the entire human life span. Erikson's model identifies prominent issues that arise
at various ages and that require resolution before one can successfully
move on. These issues are shown in Table 2.1. Most of the issues
listed in the table will be addressed at length in the chapters that follow, as will related ideas from others such as Jean Piaget[5] and Daniel
Levinson,[6] who have also utilized stage models. My purpose in pre-
senting Erikson's ideas here is to identify them as predictable psychosocial issues that involve leisure in various ways.

The *developmental task* is a useful concept for capturing the interaction of normative, age-related demands and expectations on the one
hand and individual initiative on the other. Robert Havighurst introduced this idea to identify the challenges placed before the individual
at various ages by the organism and by society.[7] The principle has
been elaborated more recently to embrace the realization that indi-

TABLE 2.1
Erik Erikson's Developmental Stages

Stage	Period	Issue
I	Infancy	Trust vs. mistrust
II	Early childhood	Autonomy vs. doubt
III	Middle childhood	Initiative vs. guilt
IV	Later childhood	Industry vs. inferiority
V	Adolescence	Identity vs. role confusion
VI	Early adulthood	Intimacy vs. isolation
VII	Middle adulthood	Generativity vs. stagnation
VIII	Later adulthood	Integrity vs. despair

viduals set their own agendas to some extent, though always with regard to other demands.[8] Tasks are defined, and actions taken and evaluated, in accordance with age-related demands and expectations.

Defining tasks and appropriating them to one's own purposes can involve both differentiation and integration. Take as an example a child's first independent trip to the neighborhood grocery store. She feels that she has reached the age and level of competence that would justify her making a case to a parent that she can walk to the store to buy some ice cream. Her parent's response reminds her of her limitations, but the task is now redefined around the conditions under which it will be permissible. The trip itself then causes her to reorganize her view of her relationship with the parent and her neighborhood and leads to the identification and differentiation of new possibilities for venturing forth into the world. As will be seen in subsequent chapters, such developmental tasks are defined and addressed throughout life.

Self-Direction and the Fourth Environment

Self-regulation and self-direction have figured prominently in developmental research and writing in recent decades, a trend reflected in the title of Lerner and Busch-Rossnagel's pioneering volume, *Individuals as Producers of Their Own Development*.[9] The extent to which individuals take action is thus regarded not only as a response to biological and social imperatives but also as a function of their own conception of alternatives.[10] Action is self-initiated and purposeful to some extent and implies a degree of freedom, personal control, and self-regulation. Such behavior is developmental to the extent that it is undertaken in the interest of becoming more of something or different in some way.

Whether prompted by the example of an admired elder, a significant life event, or other precipitating factors, individuals can author at least parts of their own life stories.[11] In *Composing a Life*, Mary Catherine Bateson discusses the lives of five prominent women as each reflects a kind of "improvisatory art . . . where familiar and unfamiliar components [are combined] in response to new situations, following an underlying grammar and an evolving aesthetic."[12] With these five women, Bateson demonstrates that even when people are determined by the actions of others, they still have the power to shape their lives in meaningful ways. Similarly, one of the leading theorists on adolescents and young adults, Norma Haan, pointed out that development follows from "curiosity and attempts to enhance life."[13]

From such observations it is clear that (1) development is an active process, not something that simply happens to someone, and (2) freedom is likely to be used to engage in activities—alone or with others—that are enjoyable and self-expanding. Rolf Oerter noted that in addition to the age-related and predictable normative tasks referred to earlier, individuals may set up *nonnormative* tasks for themselves that have the effect of *generating* development. As an example he referred to "*daseinsteigerung*," an idea previously identified by Hans Thomae, which means the "raising of existence."[14] Thomae's study group of adult respondents discussed the importance, for both the present and future, of doing such things as collecting artifacts, attending performances, and traveling.

The *personal project*, discussed by Brian Little, is a similar idea.[15] A personal project is an agenda that focuses a person's progressive adaptations to the environment. While some projects involve rather instrumental tasks such as getting a job in the "right" location or getting along better with one's brother-in-law, others involve mastering and extending leisure interests such as learning to ski or completing a music collection. Attending to such interests, taking them seriously, and developing the requisite skills and understanding to expand their scope has a "complexifying" effect on the individual. Certainly, the context of leisure affords the freedom to define and undertake personal projects.

Adolescence researchers who have used the action-in-context model[16] have referred to a *fourth environment*—beyond home, school, and work—where adult control is limited and experimentation with voluntary control is common. This context, which is essentially leisure, is especially relevant to adolescence, an idea we will consider further in Chapters 3 through 5. But the permissive qualities of the fourth environment are generally important to both differentiation and integration throughout the life span. In addition to affording an opportunity for experimentation, the time and personal space of such contexts facilitate both the interpretation of the outcomes of initial actions and the integration of their meaning within preexistent structures of understanding. Whether among adolescents congregating at a local mall or adult "regulars" at a morning coffee house, the interchange that is afforded is often a catalyst to action in other contexts.

Nonnormative developmental tasks such as the raising of existence and discretionary personal projects, then, are defined in response to factors other than age-related expectations. Self-actualization is, in fact, nonnormative development. Under ideal conditions, it unfolds in response to *growth* needs such as epistemic curiosity (the need for knowledge) rather than *deficiency* needs such as hunger or insecurity.[17] These growth needs, which also govern leisure's likely developmental uses, can be grouped under the heading of intrinsic motivation.

Intrinsic Motivation: The Push from Inside

Intrinsic motivation is the internal force that moves a person in the absence of any obvious basic homeostatic need such as hunger or any external influence or incentive. It can only be assumed when an individual asserts that the action was initiated for its own sake. According to Edward Deci and his colleagues, who have taken much of the lead in the study of the subject, intrinsic motivation arises largely in response to two prevailing organismic needs: *autonomy* and *competence*.[18] Self-determination is a synonym for autonomy, and mastery is often used as a substitute for competence. Barring the imposition of internal, deficit needs or external demands or extrinsic incentives, autonomy and competence needs direct a significant amount of human behavior, including action that may be developmentally important.

External contingencies shape socialization to a great extent. Child-rearing generally relies on "the carrot and the stick" in getting children to do what they are supposed to do and to avoid doing what they should not. Nevertheless, social involvement can be intrinsically motivated in two respects. First, it can reflect the internalization of rules and sanctions to such an extent that acting accordingly is perceived as an act of self-determination. For example, moral injunctions by parents and teachers to children that they should help their siblings and classmates may become internalized to the extent that helping others becomes "second nature," that is, intrinsically motivated.

Second, relating closely to others is itself an organismic need and thus directs action intrinsically. Social involvement, whether casual or intimate, is its own reward and directs a great deal of behavior, sometimes even in spite of external conditions. Consider, for example, the power of playmates to keep a child playing for hours on end with little regard for time or other needs.

With such inclinations in mind, intrinsic motivation researchers have added *relatedness* to competence and autonomy as intrinsic needs that direct behavior.[19] *Communion, affiliation, sociability,* and *connectedness* are other words that are commonly used to capture this aspect of intrinsic motivation. As with the other needs, the interest in relatedness is expressed differently at different ages. In Erikson's stage theory of development, intimacy is a priority of adolescents and young adults while generativity, which contributes to the growth and well-being of others, is a midlife concern. Both are age-related social constructions of the relatedness need.

Finally, though, the need for *optimal arousal* should be added to the list of intrinsic motives. Deci and Ryan subsume optimal arousal—which was a starting point for theory and research on intrinsic motivation—under the competence category. But the action orientation and self-referential qualities of the need for competence (i.e., the need to *feel* effective) are distinct from optimal-arousal needs in which response to external stimulation generates curiosity and interest without being self-referential. Optimal-arousal and competence needs may operate sequentially in some cases: incongruity and other intriguing environmental characteristics lead to interest and curiosity, which in turn generate action to create mastery of the situation. But they may operate independently as well.[20] Leisure is an ideal context for the expression of both.

Flow

When the need for competence is afforded expression, another dynamic of intrinsic motivation often results. Intense involvement, or *flow*, referred to in Chapter 1, occurs when energies and personal resources are sufficiently well matched to the challenges of a situation to elicit an extended period of rapt attention. The experience of flow has been thoroughly defined and amply elaborated by Mihaly Csikszentmihalyi and his colleagues.[21] The word *flow* was often used by those originally interviewed (it is a native, or emic, category as such) in describing their experience with the activities they most enjoyed doing. More often than not the action discussed was associated with some form of play or creative activity, including games, sports, and all manner of art forms; but people also associated it with work. In all such activities participants felt immersed in the task at hand and simultaneously challenged and in control.

The experience of flow may be the best indication of true enjoyment. Enjoyment, as discussed by Csikszentmihalyi, is distinguishable from pleasure. While the latter derives from the immediate gratification associated with meeting basic physical and sensory needs, the former reflects the positive affect associated with invested attention and sustained concentration and effort. The effort involved in flow-producing activities is not always apparent. The outward passivity of someone fishing, for example, may belie intense concentration in locating fish and attracting their attention. The lack of a response from the fish only serves to heighten the challenge—at least for a while.

This model of optimal experience, the "flow model," relies on a match between one's abilities and the challenges presented by an activity or environment. When it occurs, action and awareness merge, and self-consciousness recedes. As action and practice enhance abilities and competence, higher levels of challenge are needed to restore the flow. Performance is usually optimized under such conditions, and skills develop progressively in response to expanding challenges. Improvement in ability thus does not result from tediously practicing tasks that are mostly unappealing but from stretching to reach the next level of sustained enjoyment.

The experience of flow has been compared to Maslow's *peak experience*, which is a relatively exotic condition of intense, ecstatic enjoyment associated with acute sensation.[22] Both experiences are intense, and neither is sustainable for long. But while the progressive match between challenges and skills is difficult to orchestrate, flow is far more common in everyday life than peak experiences. While flow might be a fleeting experience for only some of the participants in an activity some of the time, it is the experience that is most often *sought* by those who choose it. And flow is cultivated by teachers and coaches who recognize its power for optimizing performance without sacrificing interest.

Intrinsically motivated behavior attracts the interest of others as well. We are intrigued by those who seem to enjoy what they are doing. And to the extent that others follow, lead, or simply share in an activity of interest, intrinsic motivation is reinforced. But if the involvement of others changes the focus from the activity to oneself, the resulting self-consciousness disrupts the concentration on the action necessary to maintain the experience. On the other hand, the awareness of self that *follows* a flow experience often includes a recognition of enhanced and extended skills and a broader reach of understanding and mastery. The sense of an enlarged and more complex self reinforces the intrinsic motivation that brought it about in the first place.

Personal Expressiveness and Social Commitment

Personal expressiveness is another product of intrinsic motivation; it is the interpretive companion of flow experience. Indeed, Alan Waterman regards them as essentially the same in many ways.[23] But according to Waterman, personal expressiveness more clearly attaches the experience to other sources of personal meaning than does flow experience. When flow-type experience is tied essentially to the realization of personal potential and the perseverance necessary to get there, it is indistinguishable from personal expressiveness and contributes most directly to self-actualization. The *purposes* individuals define for realizing their unique potentials are critical to personal expressiveness. Personal expressiveness is intense involvement that demonstrates one's *daimon*, or true calling, according to Waterman. In addition to the intensity, then, personally expressive activities create the impression that this is what one was meant to do and the feeling that this is who one really is.

Being singularly invested, emotionally and cognitively, in the task at hand, absorbed in it to the exclusion of other stimuli, is the clearest kind of intrinsically motivated activity and requires no additional reward. Such experience is tied to competence, to optimal arousal, to flow, and, if connected to personal-meaning systems, to personal expressiveness as well. But there is a social and cultural context to be recognized here, too. Whether one is playing chess, climbing a mountain, or playing fantasy games, *seriousness* about an activity forges a connection with other individuals or groups that share those interests. Specialized language, attire, and other kinds of symbols reinforce shared commitments and create the experience of being part of a defined social world. It is clearly a mode of social participation, even if the social world is fairly circumscribed in numbers, focus, and activity (a Russian literature book club, for example), perhaps known only to its members.

Interviews with musicians, collectors, amateur archaeologists, baseball players, and barbershop-quartet singers led Robert Stebbins to such conclusions about *serious leisure*.[24] The activity involvement of these devotees shows a degree of intensity that is consistent with flow experience and a pattern of commitment that joins them with others in a *unique ethos* of shared meaning and perseverance. The activities themselves take on the character of careers in many cases and are sources of self-esteem, self-actualization, and other psychological and social benefits. These are the characteristics Stebbins associates with serious leisure.

Stebbins's chief emphasis is on the identification and commitment evident in joining groups and sacrificing other aspects of life. Nevertheless, the activities that elicit this level of commitment are also likely to utilize the focused attention referred to earlier. It is this that is most critical to optimal performance, skill building, and progressive development.

Thus, intrinsic motivation, when tied with personal interest and cultivated in a context of social support for challenge-seeking and self-expansion, is directly productive of development, whether or not the activity occurs in the context of normative role expectations. But intrinsic motivation is also reflected in simple attunement to the world in which one lives; in being responsive to the available sights, sounds, and sensations; and in seeking out others in ways that may be minimally challenging but still gratifying. While we have related en-

joyment to the intense involvement of flow, enjoyment is used collo-
quially to refer to the experience of fun or pleasure as well. The context of leisure is conducive to all kinds of enjoyment.

Leisure and Development

Leisure experience relates to development in four principal ways: (1)
it is *derivative* from other developmental processes and life circumstances; (2) it is *adjustive* in allowing for some accommodation to developmental pressures and life events; (3) it is *generative* of developmental change; and (4) it is *maladaptive* in some cases, hindering
development.

Leisure Experience as Derivative

In the first of these four relationships, leisure behavior is a *result* of
developmental change. The changes in what people choose to do as
they age indicate changing issues and tasks. Many of the choices a
person makes with available free time are dictated by new-found conditions of life or emerging developmental tasks. For example, a nine-
year-old child doesn't want to accompany her parents and a younger
brother to visit her grandparents, preferring instead to join her recently acquired friends in a nearby park. Or, to establish his position
in the neighborhood, a young father agrees to provide refreshments
for a block party. Such choices are often driven by developmental
tasks and issues: for example, starting and leaving school, starting a
family and having children leave the home, and starting and leaving
work. Normative schemes of development are always a little suspect
since they are often skewed by history, culture, and even gender; nevertheless, they have heuristic value in explaining some age-related
changes in leisure behavior throughout life, a matter we will address
in the next chapter.

In addition to age-graded influences, development is also conditioned by life events—normative events, such as graduation and retirement, and nonnormative events, such as a divorce or a sudden in-
heritance.[25] Life events, both normative and nonnormative, and their
attendant social expectations and role responsibilities, have more influence on adult behavior than biological aging. This applies to leisure
behavior as well. One can expect the emergence of family leisure after
marriage and childbirth, for example, and an increase in free time at

retirement for most. But leisure may also make the life events, both predictable and unpredictable, more tolerable and manageable.

Leisure Experience as Adjustive

In the wake of developmental changes or serious life events, leisure can be a respite or a buffer. Physiologically, activities that bring about peace and relaxation are potentially restorative and therapeutic. There is curative potential in expressive activities that distract us from negative life events. Laughter may indeed be "the best medicine" in some cases. Furthermore, leisure activities are adjustive at times by providing a degree of continuity in the face of loss, as we will see in Chapter 6.

Leisure Experience as Generative

Leisure may also serve as a context for generating growth and personal transformation. As a condition of relaxed openness, it presents the opportunity for dialectical action: stabilizing integration in response to periods of change and challenging experimentation in response to periods of stability. In children experimental play differentiates in creating alternative patterns that are uniquely expressive, whereas repetitive, practice play provides an assimilating, integrative function. With advancing age the building and testing of new skills in the course of more mature self-expression contributes to an increasingly complex self.[26]

Research on the connotative meanings of leisure have demonstrated that the term is commonly associated with freedom from evaluation by others.[27] It is, as has been noted before, a context in which one can relax and feel comfortable to be oneself. Feeling like one's authentic, "true" self is common to experiences regarded as leisure and suggests an association between leisure and self-expression.[28] But the *growth* of the self, the realization of personal potential, seems to depend on taking *action* that is both personally meaningful and challenging, or, in Waterman's words, personally expressive.

Leisure's guises—derivative, adjustive, and generative—can sometimes overlap. A child's play, for example, may be an expression of a new stage of cognitive development (derivative), a way of working through fears and anxieties in play therapy (adjustive), or a bold venture into new representations of reality (generative). In some cases leisure has all three characteristics (see our studies of people with spinal cord injury in Chapter 6). By leaving one relatively unencumbered, it affords the opportunity for attunement to the environment and for exercising a multitude of developmentally responsive actions. For example, interests generated in playful experimentation may lead to patterns of investment and commitment that reorganize the self at higher levels of complexity.

The voluntary control of attention in most serious activities—whether in the context of work or leisure—enhances both enjoyment and developmental impact. Control of attention in free-time activities, as it is applied to improving competence and maintaining enjoyment, results in the kind of *self-discipline* that is necessary for success in other areas of life.[29] The ability to formulate and enact personal goals and intentions is learned most readily in contexts where "paying attention" is a matter of choice. Studies of the voluntary control of attention in adolescence indicate that those conditions are most available in structured leisure activities.[30] To the extent that such activities are valued by adult culture and represent achievement contexts that the adult culture recognizes, they offer important socialization opportunities as well.

Unfortunately, the leisure available to people is rarely used this effectively. Experience sampling studies indicate that little of the free time available to people in the United States and other Western countries is spent in generative ways.[31] Watching television, which is by far the most common leisure activity in the United States, can have both adjustive and transformative effects at times, but it acts mostly as a valve for the mere dissipation of mental energy.[32] And most other casual and social leisure activities offer little more of developmental value. Nevertheless, the relatively small percentage who do use leisure in the manner described above provide a compelling case for its potential in facilitating positive development and optimizing aging.

Leisure Experience as Maladaptive

It is tempting to argue, then, that the developmental benefits of leisure are proportional to the energy and effort expended. In other words, you get out of something what you put into it. There is, however, the prospect of *overinvestment* in leisure activity, in which case optimal psychological experience can be maladaptive developmentally. In the context of sport, for example, an athlete may be so focused as to risk premature narrowing of identity and the neglect of other developmental tasks.[33]

In some cases, too, leisure activity may be an *impediment* to developmental change—prolonged and escapist drug use is an example. Although occasional "recreational" drug use is different from habitual, hard-core use, the prospect of the former leading to the latter is sufficient reason for concern, though not the only one. Nevertheless, such activities should be considered carefully. In the case of a thirteen-year-old whose delinquent "leisure" is regarded as clearly maladaptive, the deviance may help in establishing independence, an important adolescent task.

Finally, on the negative side, the tendency to stay *busy* is a cultural pattern that might hinder the growth-producing possibilities of peaceful disengagement. Personal integration, as well as problem solving and creativity, benefit from stepping back from action and relaxing sufficiently to gain some perspective and allow new possibilities to emerge.[34] Patterns of leisure activity that have the effect of "filling" time or "getting the most out of it" obliterate the reflective value of leisure. Failure to pause and "invite the muses," as Rollo May suggests,[35] seems all too characteristic of the headlong rush of many lives, at least in the United States. Leisure activities that have the same frantic pace as the business of everyday life can never promote personal reflection.

Conclusion

In judging the value and significance of leisure experience for development, one should keep in mind the orthogenetic principles of differentiation and integration as well as the normative and nonnormative developmental tasks that individuals confront and construct for themselves. As a context of relative freedom for self-expression, leisure affords the opportunity for self-direction of personal development. Whether leisure is generative of development, however, depends primarily on whether it is used to address higher-order intrinsic needs for autonomy, competence, and/or relatedness and whether it results in feelings of personal expressiveness and social integration. Subsequent chapters will address just when and how leisure activity and experience is developmentally useful over the life span and when it is not. First, though, we will turn in the next chapter to the ways in which leisure arises from developmental changes and in that way review also the common course of development.

Notes

1. J. Brandstetter, "Action Perspectives on Human Development," in R. M. Lerner, ed., *Theoretical Models of Human Development* (New York: Wiley, 1998); R. M. Lerner and N. Busch-Rossnagel, *Individuals as Producers of Their Own Development* (New York: Academic Press, 1981); R. Silbereisen, K. Eyferth, and G. Rudinger, *Development as Action in Context: Problem Behavior and Normal Youth Development* (New York: Springer-Verlag, 1986).

2. H. Werner, "The Concept of Development from a Comparative and Organismic Point of View," in D. Harris, ed., *The Concept of Development* (Minneapolis: University of Minnesota Press, 1957).

3. See, for example, U. Bronfenbrenner, *The Ecology of Human Development* (Cambridge, MA: Harvard University Press, 1979).

4. E. Erikson, *Childhood and Society* (New York: Norton, 1962); *Identity: Youth and Crisis* (New York: Norton, 1968); *The Life Cycle Completed* (New York: Norton, 1982).

5. J. Piaget, *The Construction of Reality in the Child* (New York: Bass Books, 1954); *Play, Dreams, and Imitation in Childhood* (New York: W. W. Norton, 1962).

6. D. Levinson, C. Darrow, F. Klein, M. Levinson, and B. McKee, *The Seasons of a Man's Life* (New York: Alfred Knopf, 1978).

7. R. Havighurst, *Developmental Tasks and Education* (New York: David McKay, 1953).

8. R. Oerter, "Developmental Tasks Through the Lifespan," in P. Baltes, L. Featherman, and R. Lerner, eds., *Lifespan Development and Behavior,* vol. 7 (Hillsdale, NJ: Lawrence Erlbaum Assoc., 1986).

9. Lerner and Busch-Rossnagel, eds., *Individuals as Producers of Their Own Development.*

10. See, for example, M. Csikszentmihalyi, *The Evolving Self: A Psychology for the Third Millennium* (New York: HarperCollins, 1993); Silbereisen, Eyferth, and Rudinger, *Development as Action in Context.*

11. K. J. Kiecolt, "Stress and the Decision to Change Oneself: A Theoretical Model," *Social Psychology Quarterly* 57 (1994): 49–63; R. Helson and A. Stewart, "Personality Change in Adulthood," in T. F. Heatherton and J. L. Weinberger, eds., *Can Personality Change?* (Washington, DC: American Psychological Association, 1994); D. P. McAdams, "Can Personality Change? Levels of Stability and Growth in Personality Across the Lifespan," in Heatherton and Weinberger, eds., *Can Personality Change?*

12. M. C. Bateson, *Composing a Life* (New York: Penguin Books, 1990), 3.

13. N. Haan, "Adolescents and Young Adults as Producers of Their Own Development," in Lerner and Busch-Rossnagel, eds., *Individuals as Producers of Their Own Development*.

14. Oerter, "Developmental Tasks."

15. B. Little, "Personal Projects: A Rationale and Method for Investigation," *Environment and Behavior* 15 (1983): 273–309.

16. L. L. Caldwell, E. A. Smith, S. M. Shaw, and D. A. Kleiber, "Development as Action in Context: Active and Reactive Leisure Orientations Among Adolescents" (Paper presented at the NRPA Leisure Research Symposium, Minneapolis, 1994); R. K. Silbereisen and E. Todt, *Adolescence in Context: The Interplay of Family, School, Peers, and Work Adjustment* (New York: Springer-Verlag, 1994); W. Van Vliet, "Exploring the Fourth Environment: An Examination of the Home Range of City and Suburban Teenagers," *Environment and Behavior* 15 (1983): 567–588.

17. A. H. Maslow, *Toward a Psychology of Being*, 2d ed. (New York: Van Nostrand Reinhold, 1968).

18. E. L. Deci, *The Psychology of Self-determination* (Lexington, MA: Lexington Books, 1980); E. L. Deci and R. M. Ryan, *Intrinsic Motivation and Self-determination in Human Behavior* (New York: Plenum, 1985); E. L. Deci and R. M. Ryan, "A Motivational Approach to Self: Integration in Personality," in R. Dienstbier, ed., *Nebraska Symposium on Motivation*, vol. 38, *Perspectives on Motivation* (Lincoln: University of Nebraska Press, 1991).

19. Deci and Ryan, "A Motivational Approach to Self."

20. J. Reeve, "The Interest-Enjoyment Distinction in Intrinsic Motivation," *Motivation and Emotion* 13 (1989): 83–103.

21. M. Csikszentmihalyi, *Beyond Boredom and Anxiety* (San Francisco: Jossey-Bass, 1975); M. Csikszentmihalyi, *Flow: The Psychology of Optimal Experience* (New York: Harper Perennial, 1990); M. Csikszentmihalyi, *The Evolving Self;* M. Csikszentmihalyi and I. Csikszentmihalyi, *Optimal Experience: Psychological Studies of Flow in Consciousness* (New York: Cambridge University Press, 1988).

22. Maslow, *Toward a Psychology of Being*.

23. A. S. Waterman, "Personal Expressiveness: Philosophical and Psychological Foundations," *Journal of Mind and Behavior* 11 (1990): 47–74.

24. R. Stebbins, *Amateurs, Professionals, and Serious Leisure* (Montreal: McGill-Queen's University Press, 1992).

25. O. G. Brim and C. D. Ryff, "On the Properties of Life Events," in P. B. Baltes and O. G. Brim, eds., *Life-Span Development and Behavior*, vol. 3 (New York: Academic Press, 1980); D. R. Hultsch and J. K. Plemons, "Life

Events and Life-Span Development," in P. B. Baltes and O. G. Brim, eds., *Life-Span Development and Behavior,* vol. 2 (New York: Academic Press, 1980).

26. Csikszentmihalyi, *The Evolving Self*; Waterman, "Personal Expressiveness."

27. S. Shaw, "The Meaning of Leisure in Everyday Life," *Leisure Sciences* 13 (1985): 33–50.

28. D. M. Samdahl, "A Symbolic Interactionist Model of Leisure," *Leisure Sciences* 10 (1988): 27–39.

29. R. W. Larson, "Youth Organizations, Hobbies, and Sports as Developmental Contexts," in Silbereisen and Todt, eds., *Adolescence in Context;* R. W. Larson and D. A. Kleiber, "Structured Leisure as a Context for the Development of Attention During Adolescence," *Society and Leisure* 16 (1993): 77–93.

30. Larson and Kleiber, "Structured Leisure as a Context for the Development of Attention During Adolescence.".

31. Csikszentmihalyi, *Flow;* Csikszentmihalyi, *The Evolving Self.*

32. See, for example, R. Kubey and M. Csikszentmihalyi, *Television and the Quality of Life* (Hillsdale, NJ: Lawrence Erlbaum Assoc., 1990).

33. D. A. Kleiber and C. Kirshnit, "Sport Involvement and Identity Formation," in L. Diamant, ed., *Mind-Body Maturity* (New York: Hemisphere, 1991).

34. For further discussion of this and related ideas see, for example, D. Kleiber, "Motivational Reorientation in Adulthood and the Resource of Leisure," in D. Kleiber and M. Maehr, eds., *Motivation and Adulthood* (Greenwich, CT: JAI Press, 1985); R. Larson, "Secrets in the Bedroom: Adolescents' Private Use of Media," *Journal of Youth and Adolescence* 24 (1995): 535–550; and J. C. Robinson, *Death of a Hero, Birth of the Soul: Answering the Call of Midlife* (Tulsa: Council Oaks Books, 1993).

35. R. May, *Freedom and Destiny* (New York: W. W. Norton, 1981), 171.

3   Changes in Leisure Behavior over the Life Span

As children grow and adults age, leisure interests, activities, and meanings change. This is the *derivative* nature of leisure experience with respect to development. Changes in leisure behavior are a reflection of other developmental changes. We will address the question of the impact of leisure experience on developmental processes in subsequent chapters. Here the concern is with the changes in leisure behavior that are *predictable* over the life span. Of course, predictable changes also indicate the function and value of leisure experience as well. If the leisure of newly married couples, for example, is predictably more home-based than when the partners were single, it speaks to the effect of an important role transition; but it also hints at the significance of leisure in the establishment and maintenance of those relationships. Nevertheless, this chapter deals with the changes themselves, starting with evidence of patterns of change over the entire life span and then turning to those that apply specifically to childhood, adolescence, and adulthood.

Life Span Changes

One of the most thorough and widely cited studies of variations in leisure activity across the life span was done by Chad Gordon and his

---

Portions of this chapter appeared in chapter 9 of R. C. Mannell and D. A. Kleiber, *A Social Psychology of Leisure* (State College, PA: Venture Press, 1997). Reprinted with permission.

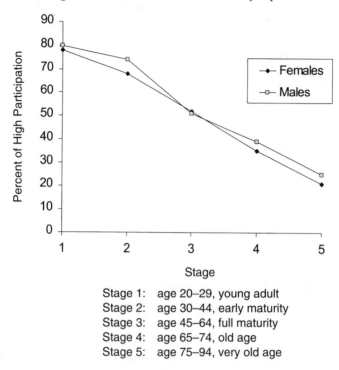

Stage 1:   age 20–29, young adult
Stage 2:   age 30–44, early maturity
Stage 3:   age 45–64, full maturity
Stage 4:   age 65–74, old age
Stage 5:   age 75–94, very old age

FIGURE 3.1
Percent of Respondents Reporting High Leisure Participation at Each of Five Stages of Adulthood

colleagues at the University of Houston with a survey of 1,441 people between the ages of twenty and ninety-four.[1] The survey was stratified according to gender, ethnicity, and two occupational statuses. This investigation showed that overall leisure activity level was negatively associated with age (see Figure 3.1), and that, with very few exceptions, most individual activities showed this same pattern. In other words, the older the person, the less likely she or he was to be found on the ski slope or in dance clubs or movie theaters, among other places. In fact, even participation in relatively sedentary activities such as socializing, playing games, and engaging in hobbies was less frequent in older age groups. Activities done outside of the home and those requiring physical exertion and high intensity of involvement showed the highest negative correlation. This negative relationship between activity and age has been shown in other studies as well.[2]

If we used the entire life span as our frame of reference, the relationship would not show such a precipitous decline. Children and adolescents must develop skills and establish some degree of independence from parents in broadening their leisure horizons. Seppo Iso-Ahola suggested a curvilinear relationship, with one's *leisure repertoire* reaching a peak in early to middle adulthood and declining thereafter[3] (although it should be pointed out that this is just what people are *able* to do rather than what they actually do, as we will see shortly). Still, it was his view that as adults age, there is a decline in the number of available personal leisure resources (i.e., skills) that corresponds to the apparent decline in the number of leisure activities in which they engage.

More recent evidence provided additional support for this general perspective. In a study of 3,927 households in Alberta, Canada, researchers found that the number of adults who indicated they had started new activities within the last year decreased steadily with each successive age group, leveling off with those who had already retired.[4] The number "replacing" activities (dropping one but starting another) also declined as a function of age. But while this research involved the respondents in considering their own changes, it is still *cross-sectional*, comparing different groups on the same behavior at the same point in time. An alternative interpretation—that different age groups may be different for other reasons, such as the experience they have shared within a cohort over time—is also possible. For example, with respect to the negative correlation between reading and age reported in the Gordon study, it may well be that the older cohorts who were surveyed *never* read as much as the younger cohorts, even when they were young. This becomes a plausible explanation when one considers the great improvements in access to education of younger cohorts compared to those born sixty years ago or more. Indeed, a more recent sixteen-year longitudinal study of a group of people over sixty showed an *increase* in reading over this period.[5] Longitudinal research is necessary to establish changes in the same individual or the same cohort over time. Longitudinal studies of the leisure patterns of older people in fact give a rather different picture than most cross-sectional studies. The prevailing evidence suggests continuity of interests rather than decline.[6] And one longitudinal study even showed an increase in activity involvement from early adulthood to middle age,[7] which might indicate a reduction in other role responsibilities.

Longitudinal studies help with the problem of interpreting change to some extent, but they still leave us with a cohort problem if we don't consider multiple cohorts at the same time. Even if a cohort has changed in a consistent way, the changes may not apply to a cohort who has had a dramatically different life history. Wars and economic depressions, for example, have clearly had an effect on the cohorts who have endured them. People who survived the depression in the late 1920s and early 1930s have been less willing to abandon themselves to immediate gratification and self-indulgence than those who have grown up with relative economic security.[8] More than any other in recent history, this cohort has been oriented toward staying busy and being productive later in life. Still other leisure-related cohort effects include the interest in music and dancing among those who grew up in the 1920s and the interest in fitness among those whose formative years included the 1960s and 1970s.[9] These interests have characterized these cohorts throughout their lives.[10]

More sophisticated studies that follow several age groups over time would offer clearer indications of the relative influence of age and history on leisure activity; but even then we would still be left with the problem of interpreting the meaning of the changes observed. Changes in overt activity can mean different things to different people. A decline in involvement in stock car racing, for example, might signal the end of interest in the activity for one person, whereas another might simply transfer his interest to some other aspect of the activity, such as teaching others to drive. Or it may be that the meanings that were sought in the activity—testing one's skills in competition, for example—are found in an alternative activity such as coaching a youth league basketball team.

Leisure researchers concern themselves primarily with changes in overt activity, but leisure interests, values, and orientations can also be influenced by developmental change. One of the orientations that apparently changes substantially over a lifetime is interest in change itself. Experimentalism is much more common among youth than among their elders. Indeed, experimentalism and an orientation to change seems to be characteristic of younger age groups. Younger cohorts must have the flexibility necessary to adapt to whatever changes come their way and to move into new niches, while older generations are responsible for providing as much stability and security in the environment as they can to afford the young a context in which to explore, experiment, and survive.[11] The well-known "generation gap"

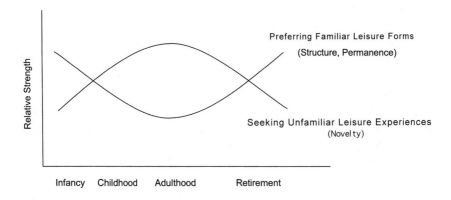

FIGURE 3.2
Relative Strength of the Tendencies to Seek Familiar and Novel Forms of Leisure Throughout the Life Span

between newer and older cohorts is partly attributable to this phenomenon. Seppo Iso-Ahola offered a hypothetical profile of the relative strength of preferences for novel versus familiar leisure forms over the life course as depicted in Figure 3.2.[12] If the suggestion is valid, older people are more like young children than young adults in their preference for familiarity.

While there are few studies that take in the entire life span, the Canadian study referred to earlier showed that over the course of four stages of adulthood, those who chose to continue with the same activities increased in number while those who started new activities decreased. The authors concluded that "the tendency to seek novelty through new leisure activities declines with advancing life stages, whereas the tendency to maintain stability through old and familiar activities increases with life stages."[13] They added, however, that this doesn't support an image of older people as disengaging entirely from activities but rather as being more selective and discriminating. Older people still have a need for stimulation and challenge for which leisure becomes ever more important, as we will see again in Chapter 8.

Studies of achievement over the life span indicate that older adults look to particular leisure activities as a way to meet achievement needs when other avenues for achievement are less available.[14] As Iso-Ahola and colleagues point out, in later life the "need for novelty may be satisfied within a narrower scope of activities" rather than by expanding the repertoire and replacing activities with new ones.[15] Nevertheless, the decline in overt experimentalism is probably adaptive in the ways discussed earlier.

Norma Haan also suggested a sequence of alterations in orientation to change and stability, based on Piaget's ideas of accommodation and assimilation.[16] The tendency to accommodate one's thinking and behavior to the realities of the external world, Haan argued, arises in later childhood, diminishes in adolescence, and reaches a high-water mark in early adulthood, when the need arises to become established. It diminishes only gradually thereafter until later life, when assimilation once again prevails. Assimilative tendencies, in contrast, are best reflected in the playfulness and internally focused reverie and storytelling that are common to childhood and old age, respectively.

The patterns of abandoning activities in later life also vary by gender. While older people are progressively less likely to participate in sports and other physically demanding forms of recreation,[17] the pattern applies most dramatically to men. Women in older cohorts today are somewhat more likely to begin new exercises than those in younger adult cohorts.[18] This same study demonstrated, however, that men in the last stages of life are more likely to begin a *wider variety* of other activities than are women. Are men inherently more experimental in later life, then? A better explanation is that retirement typically affords men more new freedoms than women. The investigators suggested that there was no real retirement for many of the women studied; the role responsibilities they had assumed for meal preparation and house maintenance did not change significantly after the age of sixty-five.

Such variations notwithstanding, leisure interests and activities are most likely to remain relatively constant over time—due less to limited opportunities for change, probably, than to a preference for maintaining old and familiar patterns. A favorite activity may be as important to hold onto as an old friend. Accordingly, much research has been devoted to the predictability of adult leisure patterns from those of childhood. Depending on how similar the behavior (e.g., fishing in lakes in childhood versus ocean fishing in adulthood), 40 percent to 80 percent of adult leisure activities have been shown to have a close equivalent form in the person's childhood.[19]

In a study using the 1982–1983 Nationwide Recreation Survey (NRS) of 6,600 people, researchers looked for evidence of *abandonment, continuity,* or *liberation* in outdoor recreation participation across the life span.[20] They found that neither the abandonment pattern, where activities are consistently given up, nor the liberation pattern, where people regularly choose new activities, show what usually happens with increasing age. Continuity is the more appropriate characterization of the activity-to-age relationship; factors other than age account for the variations in the data.

These studies demonstrate that leisure behavior is influenced by individual differences (e.g., gender), role changes (e.g., retirement), and historical changes (e.g., changing work patterns of women). Little of the change in leisure behavior over the life span is due to age alone, other than the decline in physical activity. Perhaps the most significant thing about leisure and aging is, again, the persistence of people's interests and activities.

Of course, a picture of continuity of interest and activity might obscure rather different dynamics. Is continuity the result of the enduring influence of childhood or the lack of development of adult leisure? Does one continue with an activity because of a strong commitment to the activity, with too many "side bets" to discontinue comfortably, or as a source of personal identity and self-consistency, as Robert Atchley suggests?[21] Or is an activity maintained primarily as a familiar pattern, a buffer against stress and a source of stability? Perhaps all of these apply at times. Alternatively, does change in activities reflect a response to other developmental changes, or is it a failure to find activities that are sufficiently meaningful to support a commitment and enduring involvement? In any case, studies of activity choice or consistency rarely do justice to the changes in meaning that occur across the life span. For a clearer picture we must look at some of the dynamics of development during successive periods of the life course.

Childhood: The Emergence of Leisure

When and how does a child come to see that there is time to be used at his or her discretion? We would be amused if a two-year-old responded to a request to talk to us with the words "I don't have time." We might see it as "cute," perhaps an imitation of an adult. Time pressure seems somehow incongruous with the nature of childhood. Perhaps leisure has not been studied much in childhood because it seems largely irrelevant to children's lives. Children are rarely heard to use the words *leisure* or *recreation*. Nevertheless, their ears do prick up at the sound of *play*, and they soon develop an understanding of *recess, after school, weekend*, and *vacation*.

Play and Playtime

The start of school is a line of demarcation between constraint and freedom. "Playtime," however, is an idea that most children learn before starting school as they come to distinguish it from activities like eating, cleaning up, bathing, and bedtime. Children see those activities and events as clearly within the control of parents or caregivers, and the impositions arising from them may or may not be negotiable. But a concept of leisure comparable to that of adults seems to presuppose some experience of work or at least a clear sense of the difference between free and obligated time.

Do children have anything to gain by learning to appreciate this distinction? The youngest of children tend to live in the infinite present, able to commit themselves to the moment as if nothing else mattered. Toddlers are the ultimate "leisure kind," to use deGrazia's expression,[22] since they are more likely than older people to be led by caprice. And this is not because they play—though that may be the quintessential leisure activity—but rather because, if their basic needs are met, they are very likely to be *relaxed in the present*, unconcerned about the past or future. Nevertheless, patterns of play clearly reflect changes in development, revealing the intrinsic motivations of children as they grow. Play expresses freedom for children and occupies a great deal of time for those who are afforded the requisite leeway to indulge in it. Play is not the same as exploration;[23] it is not so specifically oriented to revealing the true nature of things. It is *nonliteral* behavior, a transformation of reality (a doll represents a baby; a paper tube is a laser gun; a growl is mock anger). It is *intrinsically motivated, freely entered into*, and *actively engaging*.[24] These characteristics raise questions about the relationship between play and leisure. Leisure may or may not be taken up with active engagement, for example. But play shares the qualities of intrinsic motivation and perceived freedom with other forms of leisure, and by being transformative, it represents the qualities that make leisure different from the "paramount reality" of everyday life.[25]

As a free exercise of personal dispositions, play also provides a compelling manifestation, at least in childhood, of the essential motives and abilities of an age. Piaget pointed out that the play of infants and toddlers is generally *practice* play, reflecting the sensory-motor period of cognitive development.[26] The child exercises whatever functions he or she can to create an effect and then to make it change. Infants begin exploring and playing by putting everything into the mouth to experience it, and they repeat actions and sounds endlessly. The world of play at this time is limited primarily to the somatic self, what Erik Erikson calls the "autocosmic" sphere of the body.[27]

From the second to the fourth year, the child enters into the *microsphere*, directing attention into the near environment; here symbolic, pretend play emerges and reflects the development of representative intelligence. This stage coincides with a tremendous growth in language development.

During the first two periods play is largely private, but as children become aware of others, their play expands from the microsphere to the *macrosphere*, the world beyond the family. Initially children relate to others by playing in *parallel*, next to each other, but they eventually learn to play together in what Mildred Parten calls *associative* play.[28] In this stage they share, imitate each other, and engage in what Piaget calls *symbolic* play, pretending and exploring with new physical and social skills.[29] But children in this stage (four to seven years old) have not yet learned to decenter and take on the perspective of others. It is in the next period, from about seven to twelve, that they engage in truly cooperative play and are able to play games with rules and organize themselves collectively for other play activities.

Figure 3.3 provides a composite of the stages of play from the perspectives of Piaget, Erikson, and Mildred Parten, which highlight cognitive, psychological, and social aspects, respectively. While the ages are approximate, the functions described are thought to elicit the specified patterns of play. More will be said about these changes in Chapter 4.

Early Developmental Tasks and Leisure Experience

Leisure in childhood involves more than play, however. We might well ask the question, When do children learn to relax? Erikson's stage model of development suggests that this feeling is the best resolution of the first real issue in life, that of *trust versus mistrust*.[30] When babies become confident that their primary caregivers will return and tend to them predictably and continuously, they show signs of relax-

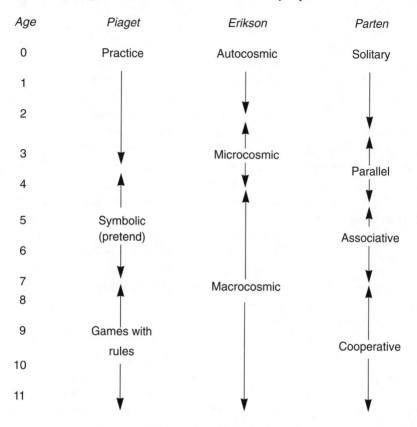

FIGURE 3.3
Play Stages

ation. This condition in turn instills the emotional security necessary for exploration, experimentation, and play. To call such a primitive emotional condition "leisure" may be a stretch; but the ability to cultivate a peacefulness about oneself throughout life may well depend on the earliest parent-child interactions.

In the next of Erikson's stages, the one-to-three year old child establishes *autonomy* and an initial sense of freedom by gaining control of vital functions and being able to say "no" and move independently of parents. This stage is a critically important antecedent to the realization of freedom in leisure later on. Failure to achieve autonomy results in a state of doubt about one's ability to be independent and self-directed that may undermine further development.[31] Exploration and experimentation are likely to be attenuated as a result.

By three or four years of age, according to Erikson, children who have successfully resolved the previous two issues begin to exercise a sense of *initiative*. Their experience when venturing out and attempting some new activity will in turn influence such risk-taking in the future. As we will see again in the next section, parents can stifle such initiative, and, according to Erikson, guilt is the prevailing response to the feeling of "overstepping one's bounds." The ability to optimize leisure, to create opportunities for enjoyment, and to be one's own source of entertainment[32] seem to rest on successfully traversing this period and overcoming such feelings.

Achieving a sense of autonomy and initiative, like establishing trust, depends on parental and family influences. Repressive, authoritarian parenting discourages autonomy and initiative. Playfulness in early childhood has been associated with parents having a flexible conceptual style and giving priority to enriching the play environment and encouraging exploration and experimentation.[33]

A liberal approach to child rearing seems to promote autonomy, initiative, play, and self-expressiveness. But laissez-faire parenting is often its own undoing. When children lack structure and predictability, trust and security are undermined, experimentation becomes less likely, and concentration is made more difficult.

Somewhere in the middle of the parenting continuum are democratic/authoritative parents who include children in decision making but establish limits and guidelines and provide some direction. This combination encourages independence while providing children with the security necessary to build confidence.[34] It may also be the best combination for realizing the full potential of leisure, as we will see shortly.

The changes in child-rearing values over the last fifty years or so have important implications for both development and leisure. A comparison of primary family values of the "Middletown" parents of fifty years ago with those of today indicates a sharp decline in the importance of obedience and a comparable increase in the importance of independence.[35] This trend might promise the emergence of an earlier appreciation of leisure, but some of this emphasis on independence results from a need to promote independence in the child while the parents work outside the home. One result of this trend, in David Elkind's view, is that contemporary children are "hurried" to grow up and, in fact, miss some of the ease and leisure of childhood.[36] Too much is expected of them too soon. According to Elkind, such children experience *responsibility overload, change overload,* and *emotional overload.* He argues further that the hurrying of children results in large part from the hurrying of parents themselves. The need to create a higher standard of living often takes precedence over leisure and relaxation and keeps even the most affluent families operating at a feverish pitch.[37]

Another symptom of the high expectations for independence in children in contemporary society is extensive television watching; an electronic form of in loco parentis, the TV as babysitter absolves the absent parents from concern about the child's activities. The time devoted to watching television in childhood, as much as thirty hours per week by some accounts,[38] precludes more active involvement in play and other leisure activities. One study found that the play behavior of a group of contemporary preschool children was significantly less social than the play norms prevalent forty years earlier, and television was considered the likeliest explanation.[39] The computer now gives children a more interactive relationship with the video monitor, whether in playing computer games or "surfing" the Internet; but the virtual sociability of computer interaction cannot substitute for real playmates.

When children have some freedom and independence and are not tethered to the television or computer, they are likely to involve siblings and peers in the creation of their own play worlds. Independence and a sense of initiative involve self-direction, and the organization of play activities gives form and action to such needs. In Erikson's view, the child's playful progression from autosphere to microsphere to macrosphere reflects a growing interest in being with others and shaping the world to his or her own purposes.[40] Venturing into the macrosphere requires (1) sufficient cognitive maturity to interact effectively with others in planning social activities such as games; (2) the initiative to create one's own opportunities for enjoyment; and (3) an underlying intrinsic interest in relatedness. When adults organize and structure children's free time, such skills and inclinations are not tested or extended.[41] And if children become accustomed to having their free time structured, they are more likely to feel bored and helpless on the rare occasions when they are unsupervised.

The desire to be part of the wider world also moves most children beyond neighborhood friends. The latter years of childhood are devoted in large part to establishing relative competence, to achieving a sense that one has and can develop skills that are well regarded by others. Being able to "produce" in one way or another results in a sense of *industry*, according to Erikson.[42] Impediments at this stage are likely to result in a prevailing sense of inferiority. In this *age of instruction*, children are attracted to groups in which they can develop skills that compare favorably with those of others—for example, the Girl Scouts, Boy Scouts, girls' and boys' clubs, youth sport teams, and 4-H Clubs. At this stage they begin to take their expressive abilities seriously in a way that is likely to define future leisure interests as well. It is, in fact, the most likely starting place for the kind of "serious leisure" that was introduced in Chapter 1.

The Age of Instruction

Children usually rely on parents and their families for guidance throughout childhood and adolescence. Nevertheless, most cultures have established practices and opportunity structures for moving children out of dependence on families and into preparation for productive membership in society. This is the essence of socialization. Ages vary, as do cultural and subcultural contexts, but as children step into school and other adult-controlled settings, they are beginning the task of separation from families that will continue into and through adolescence. The socializing systems of school and community are established in some respects to coincide with a child's natural inclination to establish competence and to connect more effectively with others. Leisure activities move away from purely child-directed play and games to activities that have some connection with the wider world. These are to be found in both school and community contexts.

The influence of schools on the development of leisure interests and orientations is inherently problematic. The knowledge base developed in schools as well as the cognitive skills associated with learning to read and write provide a strong foundation for learning activities outside of the school; but children all too often leave such interests at the schoolroom door. Most schools use an elaborate system of extrinsic motivation, primarily in the form of grades, to ensure the development of the knowledge and skills necessary for continuing on in school, for participation in the work force, and for contributing to society. But this process often undermines the intrinsic interest that children bring to learning in the same way that prizes, and other rewards, and emphasis on winning sometimes take the fun out of children's games and sports.[43] On the other hand, many schools provide exposure to a wide variety of activities in art, music, physical education, recess, and extracurricular activities.

The effects of *recess* on leisure interests and interaction patterns are particularly interesting, as well as paradoxical. An often-questioned part of the school day, these breaks are only legitimated to the extent that they support the academic objectives of the school. That is, recess has to be earned with good work in the classroom and permitted only as long as it doesn't interfere with it. There is some evidence that recess activity may even enhance classroom performance.[44] But what may be of greater value is the unique context that is created where play and social interaction can be shaped by the children within the constraints of a limited, timed break and the school playground. While children may have afternoons and weekends for self-directed activity (or to watch TV or enter into other supervised settings), the delimitation of time and space and the availability of a sizable and heterogeneous play group give recess great potential for enabling children to create their own social worlds.[45]

Municipal recreation departments, youth sport agencies, community theater, scouts, and other youth-serving agencies also provide opportunities for an enormous number of young people in the United States and Canada. Much of the initial attraction is the opportunity to join in with friends and to learn activities that are of interest to people of all ages. As was noted earlier, children in later childhood seek opportunities to develop respected skills that can be tested against and compared with those of their age mates. Instruction in activities is, at least initially, readily accepted in most cases.

The belief that such structured activities might be developmentally useful in ways that school is not makes them very popular with parents; and if a child shows some talent, he or she is often pushed along into more advanced training. But as was noted before, while this can have a positive influence on skill-building, it is a kind of "premature structuring" that makes a child a performer before he or she may be ready.[46]

Of course, opportunities for such structured experiences are not distributed evenly across all segments of society. For whatever problems overstructuring might create, there are many children who have relatively little access to structured programs of any kind. In a California study Elliott Medrich and his associates found that children from lower socioeconomic conditions, especially urban children, rarely have the provision of community services—people, places, and physical resources—that are available to more privileged children.[47] Moreover, opportunities in sports for girls and for children with disabilities lag far behind despite significant gains in recent years.

Adolescence: Finding a Self to Be Enjoyed

Many of the influences of childhood continue to direct the leisure of adolescents. Parents and peers, schools, and the world of popular culture continue to be important and become more so in some respects. In spite of the well publicized gap that exists between adolescents and other generations, adolescents invest themselves in activities established and directed by adults. They are still very willing learners and continue to seek out instruction.

But adolescence is the beginning of the end of childhood, and becoming a person in one's own right with a distinct identity is the principal task of the period. Failure to establish a sense of identity, according to Erikson, results in confusion about who one is and what one is to do. Nor does resolution of this issue happen quickly, and much exploration is needed before commitments are made.[48] In fact, as Reed Larson points out, the self of childhood must first be deconstructed in early adolescence before new conceptions of self can be entertained.[49] The adolescent sheds his or her self-image as a clinging or petulant or impulsive child as he or she seeks new levels of self-possession and independence. Creating some distance from parents and other adults—and even from peers at times—facilitates this process.

Many activities are abandoned during adolescence. In the case of sports, for example, there is an enormous dropoff in participation, especially among girls. The reasons for the decline in participation have been the subject of much research.[50] An overemphasis on winning, a lack of fun, an unwillingness to endure "schoollike" discipline, the perceived lack of ability to be competitive at a high level, the lack of social interaction with a broader range of friends outside of the sport, and growing preferences for other activities are commonly identified. But the desire to move on and away from adult direction is part of it as well. With respect to girls, there is also the view that sport involvement is inconsistent with cultivating a feminine image.

While the conflict between generations tends to be exaggerated, leisure—the "fourth environment," as it was referred to earlier—is often contested terrain. In one sense the battle is over free time itself.

Establishing emotional independence is a principal task of adolescence, and time away from home is a necessary but not sufficient condition for that; it is the way time is spent that is critically important to both parents and adolescents. Adolescents embrace leisure, whether for the freedom to sleep until noon if they please or to become experts on the latest offerings of music television. Having control over one's time and one's choices within that time brings front and center the inherent freedom of leisure.

The appropriation of adult status and privilege may also be a bone of contention. The prerogative to decide where to be—hanging out in malls, driving around late at night, and so on—is likely to be resisted by parents, by merchants who are conscious of the risk of losing customers, and by police who are aware of a direct correlation between driving late at night and criminal activities.[51] Favorite leisure activities of older adolescents—riding around in the car for fun and hanging out with friends—are prominent correlates of deviant activities.

When one considers that delinquent activities themselves may be at once enjoyable (exciting and flow-producing) and instrumental in establishing an adolescent's status with peers, their attraction is understandable. Peers often provide the appreciative audience that adolescents seek in engaging in deviant activities. The lack of an adult "guardian" reinforces a sense of freedom and independence. In a longitudinal study of 1,700 eighteen-to-twenty-six year olds, routine casual socializing behavior with peers was found to lead to increased criminal behavior, alcohol and drug use, and dangerous driving.[52] The investigators surmised that there is not much difference in offenders otherwise; many adolescents have an "openness to delinquency" that may simply lie dormant for lack of the conducive circumstances. An encouraging and idle peer group often provides such conditions, creating what Mihaly Csikszentmihalyi and Reed Larson referred to as a "deviation amplifying" effect.[53]

Even where adolescents find conditions to support more conventional opportunities, much of leisure activity is as instrumental as it is expressive. It is not what you do, but rather with whom you do it that is important. Being seen is reinforcing, and being alone is especially painful in reminding an adolescent that she or he is not being seen.

Reed Larson's experience-sampling studies with adolescents have demonstrated that being alone is associated with depressed mood—hardly a prescription for fun and enjoyment.[54] But he also found that older adolescents actually *choose* to be alone and that solitude is often used in personally expressive ways, such as writing, drawing, fantasizing about possible selves, or generating images through reading, listening to music, and just daydreaming. In this regard, Larson contrasts music listening in one's room, where the music is created by and for young people and is stimulating to one's imagination, with television watching, which features a familiar, boring adult format and is used apparently to escape stressful feelings and thoughts.[55]

The value of solitude notwithstanding, the data indicate that adolescents feel happiest when they are with others.[56] While taking a special interest in an activity and making it one's own is likely to reinforce a sense of independence and uniqueness, doing it with like-minded friends or just one significant other contributes to a sense of relatedness and even intimacy (see Chapter 4 for more on this).

The continuing development of competence in activities is itself a statement about moving into adulthood, where skills are essential for the assumption of adult roles. Whether leisure-related skills actually have any real preparation value is also addressed in the next chapter; but suffice it to say here that the fourth environment of leisure offers a range of venues for the expression of abilities and interests, from the more visible arenas of organized sports, music, and dance settings to more intimate situations such as restaurant conversations with friends. High ability per se is not required to enjoy most activities, but those that are continued through adolescence and into adulthood are likely to have two qualities: (1) they are complex enough to provide ever-increasing levels of challenge commensurate with growing skills; and (2) they include a cohort of others with similar interests, commitments, and circumstances. Such serious leisure activities remain far less common in adolescence, however, than more casual activities such as television watching and socializing.[57]

Adulthood: Role-Determined Leisure

Movement from adolescence into adulthood usually corresponds to the achievement of emotional independence from the family and a fairly stable preliminary identity structure, but there is considerably more to this transition. As noted earlier, young adults tend to be more accommodating than they were when they were younger, a trait that eases entry into the adult world. Even those who were somewhat unruly as adolescents in terms of drug and alcohol use and delinquent activities become more conventional and achievement-oriented as they move into their twenties.[58]

What leisure orientations and interests do adolescents carry with them into adulthood? Some activities may be easier than others to continue and enjoy in some fashion throughout the life course. As noted earlier, there is considerable evidence of continuity of interests and activities from childhood through adolescence and into adulthood. Some activities seem even to become leisure "careers" or avocations.[59] And perhaps these are helpful in buffering the transition into this new and challenging period. But other researchers have pointed to the *discontinuity* between childhood and adult leisure activities, with many adult activities—over 50 percent by some estimates—having no childhood antecedents.[60] New commitments—to a significant other, to colleagues at work, to a job, to a new location, for example—can lead to involvement with new activities. In spite of the evidence for consistency of leisure interests and activities, the emergence of new leisure orientations in the wake of changing life circumstances is common throughout adulthood.

In this culture the assumption of the roles of worker, spouse, and parent for those moving out of adolescence into adulthood brings dramatic changes in behavior and experience, changes reflected in leisure choices as well. As has been well established, leisure experience does not emerge in a vacuum; as free as it is, leisure is contextualized by the various roles and activities of everyday life, including those of family, work, and community life. Thus, young adults choose activities that are consistent with the new self that is being constructed in relation to those changing contexts. Leisure in fact provides free space for role interpretation beyond the requirements of parenthood, employment, or religious observance.[61] While a person may put in long hours to demonstrate commitment to the job, it is the time spent preparing a meal for people or organizing a social event for coworkers that solidifies his or her place in the organization.

Work

As adolescents and young adults take on a first full-time job, they are often astounded by how consuming it is. Eventually they adjust to the hours and establish a rhythm that allows them to anticipate "time off for good behavior." In some cases leisure is little more than a time for rest and recovery; but it is often influenced by work in more significant ways. A job brings a person into a community of coworkers or colleagues, and friendships and relationships are often extended into the context of leisure. If work is itself important enough, discussion of it may continue over dinner, at a local pub, or on the golf course. Conversely, being familiar with local sports teams or talk-show personalities often facilitates interaction with coworkers on the job. Competence in a leisure activity or the ability to converse intelligently about it may enhance one's status among coworkers, just as volunteer work may contribute to feeling a part of the community. An entry-level job offers limited opportunities for self-expression, and leisure can be used to address needs and explore interests not addressed in the workplace. Even if work is fulfilling, the intensity of it may necessitate retreat and escape in the interest of recuperation. In any case, as Daniel Levinson and others have pointed out, the transition from adolescence into the adult world must be negotiated with an awareness of gaining entry to adult society, however diverse and varied that society may be.[62] Such conventionality is not singular; the approaches to becoming established are as diverse as the surrounding cultures and subcultures. Becoming a laborer for a construction company necessitates a responsiveness to others and an attentiveness to norms of conduct that would be familiar to an initiate in a religious order.

Commitment to Another

Establishing an intimate primary relationship with another is also a principal task in the adolescent-to-adulthood transition, and being a committed partner often means tempering some values and interests to accommodate those of the other. The negotiation of discretionary patterns of activity for a couple can be a source of continued relationship development or a battleground for the preservation of self-interest and personal identity. A male acquaintance recently told me that in considering the question of marriage, he had decided that it wouldn't be enough to just do things together; more important, in his view, would be the willingness to continue to explore possibilities for new experiences together. Love is for many people a way of self-completion rather than self-sacrifice, of merging rather than matching. There is evidence, which will be reviewed in Chapter 4, that shared leisure contributes to marital success,[63] but this research only more clearly establishes what most couples suspect when they commit themselves to each other—that the stability of their relationship may depend on finding compatible patterns of enjoyment and self-expression. Such was the case of one couple who had been married for five years. Her dissatisfaction with his hunting trips (while she stayed at home) led to a threat of "finding something to do together or else." A search of local community education courses led to a wine-making class. Three years later their continuing interest in wine making—including learning to judge wines and serving as officers in a local wine-making club—is now the focal point of their shared leisure and a central life interest for both.[64]

Parenthood

Becoming a parent often entails participation in activities the child likes, albeit on the parent's terms. Relaxing and being available to children may have special advantages for developing their self-confidence, trust, and imagination, a notion we will explore in Chapter 4; but tending to their play patterns and leisure needs, often at the expense of the parent's own personal interests, seems inherent in parenthood. Leisure has special significance in family relations when parents use vacations and weekends to refine their parenting skills.[65] Family cohesiveness seems to be linked to shared leisure activities that facilitate emotional bonding, relational identification, stress management, communication skills, and feelings of support.[66] And as indicated earlier, much of what children learn to enjoy with their parents will stay with them as options throughout their lives. Parents often have some awareness of this fact and take it as their parental responsibility.

Shared play and leisure have become a more prominent part of family experience in recent years. A decline in the division of household labor and an increasing emphasis on individual expression and equity of interaction have replaced the institutional family, with its instrumental and specialized roles; in its place the "companionate" family has emerged, with its emphasis on pleasurable family interaction.[67] And in child-centered families children play a major role in shaping family leisure; indeed, they are often the "lobbyists" for particular leisure activities.[68]

Men are increasingly a part of the family leisure picture, but gender differences are still apparent. Mothers are still more likely to create the conditions for family leisure activity; and according to available evidence, they are somewhat less likely to enjoy it[69] or even to recognize it as leisure.[70] Single mothers (who greatly outnumber single fathers) and women working outside the home usually have far less freedom and fewer reprieves from parenting duties, even if there is a male partner available to assist.[71] The evidence is that there is precious little free time in such circumstances.[72] Even with husbands available, working women frequently have a "second shift" when they come home after work in tending to the family and house.[73] While the picture is changing somewhat—the nuclear family is now but one of many family patterns—leisure is still distributed unequally in most families. Full-time working men frequently expect home to be a refuge from work and are often disinclined to help out with domestic chores. Women are far more likely to feel that even if they are doing something that they want to do, they are "on duty" in taking care of the family.[74]

It has been suggested that women's leisure is different from that of men, less segmented and more integrated with their other roles.[75] Nevertheless, the reality for mothers of adolescent children, according to experience-sampling data from middle- and working-class families, is that while they may be fundamentally fulfilled in parental roles, women experience little of the sense of freedom and enjoyment at home that is usually associated with leisure.[76] The women participating in this study had a general "leisure-lack," with little time for themselves and few reports of the freedom, relaxation, or positive affect generally associated with leisure. Instead, their greatest enjoyment was found outside the home in conversational relationships with friends and colleagues. By contrast, men experienced their most positive, relaxed, enjoyable circumstances at home, even if this involved some degree of housework and child care, because they experience such duties as voluntary.

Midlife Changes

Midlife typically brings a variety of changes for people. The work roles that people have been committed to often lose their importance, and novel challenges arise as children leave home. While there is still tremendous variation in the complexity of work and family life in this age group, more free time and greater financial security often provide ideal conditions for self-expression in leisure at this time. But the first signs of aging—loss of youthful appearance or health problems—are likely to lead to an awareness of one's mortality and create a sense of urgency about life. A very hardworking colleague of mine was recently diagnosed with a serious illness. Among her responses was to go out and buy that grand piano she had been wanting and "to take every opportunity to hug [her] grandbabies." Even for those with larger amounts of time and money, time is likely to become a more precious commodity. As Bernice Neugarten and others have noted, time orientation changes from years-since-birth to years-left-to-live.[77] Furthermore, the emphasis on establishing oneself in the earlier years is likely to have promoted certain characteristics—such as competitiveness in the case of many men and nurturance in the case of women—at the expense of others. Leisure, then, is likely to be seen as an opportunity to explore those neglected aspects of oneself.

Take the example of a forty-seven-year-old private school teacher who was passed over for the position of principal. The ensuing disillusionment caused him to reconsider how he spent his time and what brought him the most enjoyment and satisfaction. He turned to his home office to complete a photo display for the family and resumed an interest in a music collection that he had neglected. There are many such examples of people who come to an awareness that they have been chasing a dream or have been locked into a job or a family situation and almost welcome a life-changing catalyst. Just how such changes contribute to development is considered further in Chapter 7.

Retirement

The *interest* in making lifestyle changes at midlife may go unrealized for lack of opportunity; the requirements of work or family responsibilities continue for most people. Aging parents, for example, may replace children as a focus of concern. And in the case where a job has been lost, the sudden abundance of "free" time does not compensate for the lost income and status. Retirement, however, is dramatically different from unemployment—it usually connotes the earned privileges of not working and the freedom of indulging one's yearnings for more personally edifying activities. Most people look forward to retirement; having "paid their dues" for many years, they see it as the time to finally do those things they have been putting off, though disposable income will determine their ability to do so. Thanks to longer life expectancies, retirement often leads to a period of exploration and self-expansion, at least until health problems interfere. The possibility of more complete immersion in activities such as traveling and hobbies offers the prospect of a deeper level of enjoyment and satisfaction—for example, designing and completing a brick patio or enrolling in an elder hostel program can bring about a sense of competence that may have been threatened in the final years of work, where one might have been considered "over the hill" or "dead wood." In addition, opportunities for volunteer work and other kinds of community service become less obligatory and therefore more attractive.

Once again, however, such options and patterns are a function of class and gender differences. As we noted earlier, women who follow husbands into retirement are likely to realize fewer rewards as they proceed with "business as usual" in managing and maintaining the home.

Grandparenthood

Becoming a grandparent has a very different impact on leisure experience than becoming a parent. Caring for grandchildren can be done more expressively (except for grandparents who find themselves with primary child care duties) than was the case in parenting one's own children. As they age, grandparents often become advocates for enjoying life more. In approaching the end of the road, they are regularly reminded that the journey is the important thing and that the present should not be wholly sacrificed for the future. These are also the circumstances for demonstrating a degree of wisdom and a variety of ways of caring.[78]

Loss of a Spouse

The expanded role of grandparent contrasts with the constriction occasioned by the loss of a spouse or close friends. A loss of leisure often accompanies such changes. But the loss of a spouse is so predictable in later life it is appropriate to consider it here as a part of the normal aging process. The loss of shared leisure may mean the loss of companionship altogether. Married people have been found to have a narrower range of activities than single people,[79] and so the loss of a spouse may be particularly consequential for those who have done things mostly together. On the other hand, the loss can also have a liberating effect, especially in the case where the spouse was overbearing and determining. In such cases a kind of blossoming of self-expression often follows, with leisure taking on special new meaning.

Negative Life Events

To understand development it is important to understand both change and continuity. In this chapter we have been concerned mostly with predictable change, whether through role changes or the tasks that come with a particular period in life. But many of the changes people make arise from *unpredictable,* disruptive events such as divorce or loss of a limb. While it may be important in transcending the event, leisure is often prominent in that which *defines* the event. A disability, for example, includes the loss of sources of pleasure, enjoyment, and self-expression.[80] One grieves for those things as part of the self that must be relinquished. With such events come two competing tendencies: (1) the readiness for experimentation/differentiation (the events themselves are turning points) and (2) the need for continuity/familiarity to stabilize oneself. Continuity of interests should not be taken as a lack of development, however, since the change created by the event itself requires integration and assimilation, a kind of "restorying." In such cases it is clear that life has changed dramatically.

Conclusion

If leisure is the *product* of developmental changes, it is also a reliable marker of such changes. From childhood to old age, the ways in which people define and use their freedom reveal much about who they are. There are important distinctions between the ages, however: the maturation process of youth, while largely socially directed, appears to unfold in play and self-expressive activities; the tasks that confront adolescents and young adults prepare them for the world ahead and circumscribe leisure activities accordingly. Changes in the leisure activities and experiences of adults demonstrate in turn the impact of social roles on the individual as well as the need to resist, manage, and ultimately relinquish them. To see leisure only as a product of developmental change or as a kind of shock absorber, however, is to miss its full significance, as the following chapters will show.

Notes

1. C. Gordon, C. Gaitz, and J. Scott, "Leisure and Lives: Personal Expressivity Across the Lifespan," in R. H. Binstock and E. Shanas, eds., *Handbook of Aging and the Social Sciences* (New York: Van Nostrand-Reinhold, 1976).

2. For example, J. R. Kelly, *Peoria Winter: Styles and Resources in Later Life* (Lexington, MA: Heath, 1987); M. Unkel, "Physical Recreation Participation of Females and Males During the Adult Life Cycle," *Leisure Sciences* 4 (1994): 29–49.

3. S. E. Iso-Ahola, *Social Psychology of Leisure and Recreation* (Dubuque, IA: W. C. Brown, 1980).

4. S. E. Iso-Ahola, E. Jackson, and E. Dunn, "Starting, Ceasing, and Replacing Leisure Activities over the Lifespan," *Journal of Leisure Research* 26 (1994): 227–249.

5. D. Stanley and V. Freysinger, "The Impact of Age, Health, and Sex on the Frequency of Older Adults' Leisure Activity Participation: A Longitudinal Study," *Activities, Adaptation, and Aging* 19 (1995): 31–42.

6. S. J. Cutler, "Aging and Voluntary Association Participation," *Journal of Gerontology* 32 (1977): 470–479; J. W. Lounsbury and L. L. Hoopes, "Five Year Stability of Leisure Activity and Motivation Factors," *Journal of Leisure Research* 20 (1988): 118–134; E. Palmore, *Social Patterns in Normal Aging* (Durham, NC: Duke University Press, 1981); R. Schmitz-Scherzer, "Longitudinal Change in Leisure Behavior of the Elderly," *Contributions to Human Development* 3 (1976): 127–136; D. Scott and F. Willits, "Adolescent and Adult Leisure Patterns: A 37-year Follow-up Study," *Leisure Sciences* 4 (1989): 323–336.

7. V. Freysinger and R. Ray, "The Activity Involvement of Women and Men in Young and Middle Adulthood: A Panel Study," *Leisure Sciences* 16 (1994): 193–217.

8. For more on this point see G. Elder, *Children of the Great Depression* (Chicago: University of Chicago Press, 1974).

9. B. McPherson, *Aging as a Social Process* (Toronto: Butterworth, 1990).

10. The meaning of leisure itself is historically situated, as I suggested in the preface and as Christopher Rojek has argued in a critique of contemporary leisure theorists and researchers. (C. Rojek, "De-differentiation and Leisure," *Society and Leisure* 16 [1993]: 15–29.) Rojek pointed to the tendency of this group to idealize leisure as something separate from and superior to work or other contexts. This is a fiction, or "dreamworld" as he calls it, that fails to recognize the influence of market forces in creating leisure "needs" and the extent to which enjoyment is found in negative and antisocial activities.

11. S. Brent, "Individual Specialization, Collective Adaptation and Rate of Environmental Change," *Human Development* 21 (1978): 33.

12. Iso-Ahola, *Social Psychology of Leisure and Recreation.*

13. Iso-Ahola, Jackson, and Dunn, "Starting, Ceasing, and Replacing Leisure Activities over the Lifespan," 243.

14. J. Veroff and D. A. Smith, "Motives and Values over the Adult Years," in D. A. Kleiber and M. Maehr, eds., *Motivation and Adulthood* (Greenwich, CT: JAI Press, 1985).

15. Iso-Ahola, Jackson, and Dunn, "Starting, Ceasing, and Replacing Leisure Activities over the Lifespan," 245.

16. N. Haan, "Adolescents and Young Adults as Producers of Their Own Development," in R. Lerner and N. Busch-Rossnagel, eds., *Individuals as Producers of Their Own Development* (New York: Academic Press, 1981).

17. Gordon, Gaitz, and Scott, "Leisure and Lives"; Kelly, *Peoria Winter*; Unkel, "Physical Recreation Participation of Females and Males During the Adult Life Cycle."

18. Iso-Ahola, Jackson, and Dunn, "Starting, Ceasing, and Replacing Leisure Activities over the Lifespan."

19. F. McGuire, F. Dottavio, and J. O'Leary, "The Relationship of Early Life Experiences to Later Life Leisure Involvement," *Leisure Science* 9 (1987): 251–257; A. J. Sofranko and M. F. Nolan, "Early Life Experience and Adult Sports Participation," *Journal of Leisure Research* 4 (1972): 6–18; D. R. Yoesting and J. E. Christensen, "Re-examining the Significance of Childhood Recreation Patterns on Adult Leisure Behavior," *Leisure Sciences* 1 (1978): 219–229.

20. F. McGuire and F. Dottavio, "Outdoor Recreation Participation Across the Lifespan: Abandonment, Continuity, or Liberation?" *International Journal of Aging and Human Development* 24 (1987): 87–99; See also M. S. Searle, J. E. Mactavish, and R. E. Braley, "Integrating Ceasing Participation with Other Aspects of Leisure Behaviour," *Journal of Leisure Research* 25 (1993): 389–404.

21. R. C. Atchley, "Continuity Theory and the Evolution of Activity in Later Life," in J. R. Kelly, ed., *Activity and Aging* (Thousand Oaks, CA: Sage, 1993).

22. S. deGrazia, *Of Time, Work, and Leisure* (New York: Anchor, 1962).

23. J. Piaget, *Play, Dreams, and Imitation in Childhood* (Boston: Beacon, 1962); C. Hutt, "Exploration and Play in Children," in R. Herron and B. Sutton-Smith, eds., *Children's Play* (New York: Wiley, 1971).

24. In M. J. Ellis, *Why People Play* (Englewood-Cliffs: Prentice-Hall, 1973); F. P. Hughes, *Children, Play, and Development* (Needham Heights, MA: Allyn and Bacon, 1991); J. Huizinga, *Homo Ludens* (Boston: Beacon Press, 1955); and H. Schwartzman, *Transformations: The Anthropology of Children's Play* (New York: Plenum Press, 1978), among many other books on play, the authors provide defining elements, some in common, some different.

25. I have discussed this idea elsewhere ("Motivational Reorientation in Adulthood and the Resource of Leisure," in D. Kleiber and M. Maehr, eds., *Motivation and Adulthood* [Greenwich, CT: JAI Press, 1985]). In *Capitalism and Leisure Theory* (London: Tavistock, 1985) Christopher Rojek takes a quite different position, arguing that play differs from leisure primarily in the absence of self-consciousness, which is ever present in the latter. However, while much of leisure does involve an awareness of self, it is eliminated when flowlike involvement and playlike absorption are achieved.

26. J. Piaget, *Play, Dreams, and Imitation in Childhood.*

27. E. Erikson, *Childhood and Society* (New York: Norton, 1963), 220.

28. M. Parten, "Social Play Among Preschool Children," *Journal of Abnormal and Social Psychology* 28 (1932): 136–147.

29. Piaget, *Play, Dreams, and Imitation in Childhood.*

30. Erikson, *Childhood and Society.*

31. Ibid., 251–253.

32. R. Mannell, "Personality in Leisure Theory: The Self as Entertainment Construct," *Society and Leisure* 7 (1984): 229–242.

33. D. W. Bishop and C. Chace, "Parental Conceptual Systems, Home Play Environment, and Potential Creativity in Children," *Journal of Experimental Child Psychology* 12 (1971): 218–338; J. N. Liebermann, *Playfulness: Its Relationship to Imagination and Creativity* (New York: Academic Press, 1977).

34. D. Baumrind, "Some Thoughts About Child Rearing," in S. Cohen and T. J. Comiskey, eds., *Child Development: Contemporary Perspectives* (Itasca, IL: F. E. Peacock, 1977).

35. T. Caplow, H. M. Bahr, B. A. Chadwick, R. Hill, and M. H. Williamson, *Middletown Families* (Minneapolis: University of Minnesota Press, 1982).

36. D. Elkind, *The Hurried Child* (Boston: Addison-Wesley, 1981).

37. See also S. Linder, *The Harried Leisure Class* (New York: Columbia University Press, 1971).

38. For example, J. P. Tangney and S. Feshbach, "Children's Television Viewing Frequency," *Personality and Social Psychology Bulletin* 14 (1988): 145–158.

39. K. Barnes, "Preschool Play Norms: A Replication," *Developmental Psychology Monographs* 1 (1970): 99–103.

40. E. Erikson, *Childhood and Society,* 209–222.

41. E. Devereux, "Backyard Versus Little League Baseball: The Impoverishment of Children's Games," in D. Landers, ed., *Social Problems in Sport* (Urbana, IL: University of Illinois Press, 1976); D. Kleiber and L. Barnett, "Leisure in Childhood," *Young Children* 35(5) (1980): 47–53.

42. Erikson, *Childhood and Society,* 252.

43. M. Lepper and D. Greene, eds., *The Hidden Costs of Rewards* (New York: Wiley, 1978).

44. A. D. Pellegrini and P. K. Smith, "School Recess: Implications for Education and Development," *Review of Educational Research* 63 (1993): 51–67; J. Evans, *Children at Play: Life in the School Playground* (Geelong, Australia: Deakin University Press, 1989).

45. Evans, *Children at Play.*

46. Elkind, *The Hurried Child.*

47. E. Medrich, J. Roizen, V. Rubin, and S. Buckley, *The Serious Business of Growing Up: A Study of Children's Lives Outside of School* (Berkeley: University of California Press, 1982).

48. J. Marcia, "Identity in Adolescence," in J. Adelson, ed., *Handbook of Adolescent Psychology* (New York: Wiley, 1980).

49. R. Larson, "Secrets in the Bedroom: Adolescents' Private Use of Media," *Journal of Youth and Adolescence* 24 (1995): 535–550.

50. See, for example, J. E. Curtis and P. T. White, "Age and Sport Participation: Decline in Participation or Increased Specialization with Age?" in N. Theberge and Donnelly, eds., *Sport and the Sociological Imagination* (New York: TCU Press, 1984); C. E. Kirshnit, M. Ham, and M. H. Richards, "The Sporting Life: Athletic Activities During Adolescence," *Journal of Youth and Adolescence* 18 (1986): 601–616.

51. D. W. Osgood, J. K. Wilson, P. M. O'Malley, J. G. Bachman, and L. D. Johnston, "Routine Activities and Individual Deviant Behavior," *American Sociological Review* 61 (1996): 635–655.

52. Ibid.

53. M. Csikszentmihalyi and R. Larson, *Being Adolescent* (New York: Basic Books, 1984).

54. R. Larson, "The Solitary Side of Life: An Examination of the Time People Spend Alone from Childhood to Old Age," *Developmental Review* 10 (1990): 155–183.

55. Larson, "Secrets in the Bedroom."

56. Csikszentmihalyi and Larson, *Being Adolescent.*

57. Ibid.

58. R. Jessor, J. E. Donovan, and F. M. Costa, *Beyond Adolescence: Problem Behavior and Young Adult Development* (New York: Cambridge University Press, 1991).

59. R. A. Stebbins, *Amateurs, Professionals, and Serious Leisure* (Montreal: McGill-Queen's University Press, 1992).

60. J. R. Kelly, "Socialization Toward Leisure: A Developmental Approach," *Journal of Leisure Research* 6 (1974): 181–193; "Leisure Socialization: Replication and Extension," *Journal of Leisure Research* 9 (1977): 121–132.

61. J. R. Kelly, *Freedom to Be: A New Sociology of Leisure* (New York: Macmillan, 1987).

62. D. Levinson, C. Darrow, F. Klein, M. Levinson, and B. McKee, *The Seasons of a Man's Life* (New York: Knopf, 1978).

63. D. K. Orthner, L. Barnett-Morris, and J. A. Mancini, "Leisure and the Family over the Life Cycle," in L. L'Abate, ed., *Handbook of Developmental Family Psychology and Psychopathology* (New York: Wiley, 1992).

64. This case was described to me by a colleague.

65. Kelly, *Freedom to Be.*

66. Orthner, Barnett-Morris, and Mancini, "Leisure and the Family."

67. Ibid.

68. D. R. Howard and R. Madrigal, "Who Makes the Decision: The Parent or the Child? The Perceived Influence of Parents and Children on the Purchase of Recreation Services," *Journal of Leisure Research* 22 (1990): 244–258.

69. R. W. Larson and M. H. Richards, *Divergent Realities: The Emotional Lives of Mothers, Fathers, and Adolescents* (New York: Basic Books, 1994); S. M. Shaw, "Gender in the Definition and Perception of Household Labor," *Family Relations* 37 (1988): 333–337.

70. S. M. Shaw, "Dereifying Family Leisure: An Examination of Women's and Men's Everyday Experiences and Perceptions of Family Time," *Leisure Sciences* 14 (1992): 271–286.

71. Larson and Richards, *Divergent Realities.*

72. Shaw, "Dereifying Family Leisure."

73. A. R. Hochschild, *The Second Shift* (New York: Avon, 1989).

74. Larson and Richards, *Divergent Realities*; Shaw, "Dereifying Family Leisure."

75. L. Bella, "Women and Leisure: Beyond Androcentrism," in E. L. Jackson and T. L. Burton, eds., *Understanding Leisure and Recreation: Mapping the Past, Charting the Future* (State College, PA: Venture Publishing, 1989).

76. Larson and Richards, *Divergent Realities.*

77. B. Neugarten, "Personality and Aging," in J. Birren and K. W. Schaie, eds., *Handbook of the Psychology of Aging* (New York: Van Nostrand Reinhold, 1977).

78. J. C. Robinson, *Death of a Hero, Birth of the Soul: Answering the Call of Midlife* (Tulsa: Council Oaks Books, 1993).

79. T. Holman and A. Epperson, "Family and Leisure: A Review of the Literature with Research Recommendations," *Journal of Leisure Research* 16 (1984): 277–294.

80. D. A. Kleiber, S. C. Brock, J. Dattilo, Y. Lee, and L. Caldwell, "The Relevance of Leisure in an Illness Experience: Realities of Spinal Cord Injury," *Journal of Leisure Research* 27 (1995): 283–299.

4 Socialization Through Play and Leisure Activity

In every culture child-rearing rules are viewed as standards by parents and as constraints by children. The premise of this chapter is that leisure can mediate an essential dialectical opposition: if the child's self-interest prevails, social learning and social integration can suffer; if, on the other hand, children are oversocialized, self-expression is at risk. Critical theory reminds us that simply perpetuating social processes reproduces the bad as well as the good. Cultural evolution is a matter of change, and leisure, where self-expression leads to new possibilities, has a role to play in generating that change.[1]

We will give fuller attention to the creative power of leisure experience in the next chapter, where we will consider differentiation and individuation in identity formation, but it is important to recognize it here as a vector in the dialectic of socialization. Leisure also facilitates the antithesis, social and cultural integration, as evidenced by the popular acceptance of extracurricular and other organized leisure activities. This chapter focuses on the expressive behavior that promotes the social skills necessary for full participation in society.

Socialization

An understanding of socialization depends on the disciplinary perspective used. Sociology, psychology, political science, and anthropology approach the topic somewhat differently. Our more psychological ap-

---

Portions of this chapter appeared in chapter 8 of R. C. Mannell and D. A. Kleiber, *A Social Psychology of Leisure* (State College, PA: Venture Press, 1997).

proach represents the idea in terms of the developmental tasks introduced in Chapter 2. Most developmental tasks are defined by society—developing writing skills, for example—but some are defined by individuals. Socialization is what we do to guide, train, or indoctrinate children, but people of all ages also *self-socialize*, identifying their own tasks in the interest of integrating into the world. As children age, the locus of socialization moves from parents to those outside the family in schools and community centers to individuals themselves. But even in the youngest children there is evidence of self-socialization as they take steps to gain competence in ways that bring the world to them. The literature on socialization has focused mostly on the external influences that shape and regulate child and adolescent behavior, but self-direction and intrinsic motivation interact with those external forces.[2]

Developmental Tasks

Developmental tasks are regarded, both by the individual and social institutions, as the steps required to make one's way in life. These steps have been outlined in the past,[3] but they are modified as societies change over time. In the 1950s Robert Havighurst identified them (see Table 4.1) as the tasks of that period for successive age groups. Most of these would still apply in much of Western society, albeit with some updating of the language, but others, such as "learning appropriate masculine and feminine social roles," would lack the same consensus they had earlier.

The developmental issues identified by Erik Erikson, introduced in Chapters 2 and 3, also define challenges that may be regarded as tasks, and so they are listed in Table 4.1 as well. The tasks are negotiated as an interaction of self-direction and environmental influence. For example, when a parent offers to help a child learn to ride a bike and negotiate the neighborhood, the gesture may or may not be a response to the child's own *initiative*. But the skills acquired by the child identify him or her as one who is "able" and thus reinforces a sense of competence or *industry*, to use Erikson's term. From adolescence onward, parents and other caregivers are less likely to influence task definition for resolving the sequence of developmental issues discussed by Erikson and others. Nevertheless, even the tasks of middle age come to be interpreted in relation to social contexts.

Parents, teachers, siblings, and older children regularly present developmental tasks; but individuals exercise control in addressing and

TABLE 4.1
Developmental Tasks

Period	Havighurst's Tasks	Erikson's Issues
Infancy	Learning to walk, eat, and talk Learning to control elimination	Trust vs. mistrust
Early childhood	Learning sex differences and modesty Forming concepts and learning language	Autonomy vs. doubt
Middle childhood	Getting ready to read Learning to distinguish right from wrong	Initiative vs. guilt
Later childhood	Learning skills necessary for games Building wholesome attitude toward self Learning appropriate masculine and feminine social roles Developing academic skills Developing concepts necessary for everyday living Developing conscience, morality, and a scale of values Achieving personal independence Developing attitudes toward social groups and institutions	Industry vs. inferiority
Adolescence	Achieving new relations with age mates Achieving masculine and feminine social roles Accepting one's physique Achieving emotional independence of adults Preparing for marriage and family life Preparing for an economic career Developing an ideology Achieving socially responsible behavior	Identity vs. role confusion
Early adulthood	Selecting a mate Learning to live with a marriage partner Starting a family Rearing children and managing a home Getting started in an occupation Taking civic responsibility Finding a congenial social group	Intimacy vs. isolation
Middle adulthood	Assisting children to become adults Achieving adult social responsibility Reaching satisfactory career performance Developing adult leisure-time activities Relating to one's spouse as a person Adjusting to physiological changes Adjusting to aging parents	Generativity vs. stagnation
Later adulthood	Adjusting to declining strength and health Adjusting to retirement and reduced income Adjusting to death of a spouse Establishing affiliation with age group Adapting social roles in a flexible way Establishing satisfactory living conditions	Integrity vs. despair

interpreting them. As such they become "producers of their own development."[4] In fact, individuals come to define their own tasks and projects to the extent that they are adequately prepared psychologically and sufficiently advantaged socially.

Conflicts inevitably arise, however, whether from the perspective of society or that of the developing individual. The tasks of emotional, social, and moral development are not always compatible. For example, an achievement orientation may be inconsistent at times with generosity; and acting morally may threaten social integration if doing so risks rejection and ridicule by one's peer group. Leisure experiences exert both positive and negative influence in all of these areas.

Leisure and Self-Socialization

Developing children are largely self-socializing, though not yet in the full self-conscious sense of adolescents. This process involves leisure in three important ways: (1) if leisure leads to play, children are likely to benefit cognitively, physically, socially, and emotionally; (2) social activities that are enjoyable and personally expressive are likely to lead to other more instrumental age-appropriate activities; and (3) voluntary and enjoyable social activities—scouting, clubs, youth sports, festivals, or cultural rituals, for example—promote social integration.[5]

Csikszentmihalyi pointed out that expressive activities come "ontogenetically prior" to instrumental ones.[6] In other words, children readily take more seriously those activities that they initially enjoy and that offer them incremental challenges. And if the activities involve others and are formally organized in some way, they serve as an entrée into the wider culture.[7] For example, the sixteen-year-old son of a friend developed a collection of baseball cards that he brought as trading material to hobby fairs. He studied their value and engaged others, mostly adults, in trades. In the process he developed his ability to negotiate his interests with other hobbyists, young and old. Deciding to master a musical instrument is another example. What starts out as playful experimentation is gradually recognized as a subject worthy of sustained attention.

Children are more likely to take activities seriously as they get older, but at least as often activities serve merely as vehicles for facilitating and defining social interaction. A number of the developmental tasks of childhood and adolescence have to do with learning to interact effectively with others (see Table 4.1). Initially, children seek out others in self-directed activities—to come out to play, to "sleep over," and so on. Later, more formally organized activities allow preadolescents opportunities to create some shared involvement or actually to make new friendships. Finally, though, the activity may be largely irrelevant as adolescents look for opportunities to be part of a peer culture. Expressive interests—for example, in music, styles of dress, adornment, and so on—define the groups one seeks to join. These patterns and interests are expressed in the context of leisure as well as in schools and elsewhere. While more serious, structured activities such as music, sports, and hobbies may bring adolescents together, the "casual" leisure of informal socializing is far more common and popular as a context for connecting with others and, through display of similar tastes and interests, establishing membership in particular cliques and subcultures. Indeed, adolescents think of leisure as mostly a matter of relaxation and casual social interaction.[8] However, the fact that such situations are relatively ambiguous and unstructured opens the door for virtually anything, including deviant and delinquent activities.

Partly as a result of a concern that "idle hands are the devil's workbench" and a belief in the power of organized activities, adults are predisposed to favor structured, supervised activities over self-directed ones. Seeing their socializing potential, parents and other adults often take advantage of leisure opportunities and activities to teach children important skills and values or to have others do so. Leisure itself may be at risk here, as freedom and spontaneity give way to expectations for learning and performance, pressures which usually come in direct proportion to the extent to which adults are involved. And it is relatively easy for adults to undermine the intrinsic motivation that makes an activity attractive in the first place by offering unnecessary rewards or unwanted praise or criticism.[9] But this is not to say that children naturally resist and deplore structure. Children and adolescents often pursue opportunities structured by others to deepen involvement, hone their skills, and form enduring play/work relationships. The sacrifice of some amount of self-direction for the opportunity to enrich one's experience seems a fair exchange in most cases, especially where self-enhancement is the expected outcome of such involvement.

The Power of Play

Play is the forerunner of much of the leisure behavior that occurs over the life span. Children play well before they come to appreciate leisure (or free time, playtime, recess, and the like) as a province of preferred experience. Developing a concept of leisure involves a certain amount of self-consciousness about such things, and this self-consciousness develops only with the maturity of later childhood. Intentionally chosen leisure activities offer opportunities for socialization; but because they are both socially constructed and embedded in the social contexts of family, school, and community, they usually come with a heavy dose of social control as well. How well such activities actually facilitate movement through childhood and adolescence varies with the context, the dimension of socialization, and the nature of the experience that the activity affords. The underlying potential of such activities, however, is most clearly revealed in the dynamics of children's play.

The study of play offers a good starting place because play demonstrates the power of intrinsic motivation in directing growth-producing interactions with the physical and social environment.[10] Because the consequences of play are unimportant in the immediate sense, the player has the opportunity to test limits with relative impunity, focusing only on the quality of the experience itself. Paradoxically, the attendant risk-taking promotes the elaboration of functions and skills that are ultimately useful.[11] A child who playfully sends a computer message to a friend and eagerly anticipates a response learns about the friend, the properties of the technology, and his or her own abilities. The Russian psychologist Leonid Vygotsky was especially impressed with the importance of play in learning and development as a mechanism for anticipating the next level of maturity.[12]

Piaget argued that play is the subordination of accommodation to assimilation; incorporating thoughts and images into one's existing ways of thinking (assimilation) is more important in play than reorganizing ways of thinking to bring them in line with external realities (accommodation). Play has a Dionysian character, entertaining the unbridled and the uncivilized in the interest of manipulating the world to its own design. While this tendency can be a source of creativity, it can also lead to deviance of one kind or another. Indeed, the tendency to idealize and romanticize play must be tempered with the realization that playful impulses may be "dirty," antisocial, degenerate and even destructive.[13] Torturing the cat may be great sport for a couple of five-year-olds.

Such tendencies don't disappear with age. Schechner's analysis of "dark play" uses the example of a woman who enjoyed dancing on the edge of precipices in spite of the horrified reactions of family and friends.[14] But children do develop with age at least the capacity to modulate assimilative tendencies in play, if only for the purposes of incorporating others into their play world. This was evident to Erikson in children's movement in play from the autosphere of self to the microsphere of the immediate environment to the macrosphere of the social world beyond.[15] Indeed, play has been discussed as a means of preparation for adulthood, a kind of "anticipatory socialization."[16] Children play the roles of adulthood—mothers, doctors, teachers—thus developing some command over the roles as they move into a better position to engage the outside world.

Not surprisingly, there is little evidence that children play intentionally to prepare themselves for the future; children are present-centered in their play. Nevertheless, the developmental advantages of play are sufficient to persuade parents and educators to go to great lengths to facilitate it. Formalizing and structuring play and other activities may create certain problems, including the possibility of undermining the play spirit in the activity, but taking such activities seriously brings other advantages.

Structured Activities and Serious Leisure

Leisure in childhood and adolescence is informal and casual for the most part. Spontaneous play and television watching in childhood and "hanging out" and talking on the phone in adolescence far exceed involvement in organized activities. But structured activities are important for two reasons: (1) they represent an enormous investment of adult society in providing opportunities and environments for instruction and performance; and (2) they offer the greatest potential for the widest range of developmental impacts. Becoming seriously involved in an activity with others is a way of participating in the society at large, even if the social world of a particular activity is fairly confined. Serious leisure activities are sufficiently demanding to offer a pathway to the social world of adults. When a budding amateur astronomer shares that interest with her father, an older sister, or the club leader, she envisions a future of opportunities for progressively more challenging involvement.[17]

The same characteristics of perseverance and focused attention might be found in job opportunities; but most of the work opportunities children and adolescents have are not particularly demanding or emotionally satisfying,[18] whereas many serious leisure activities are. In such activities participants learn to concentrate and put forth effort, behaviors generally associated with work, with no cost to enjoyment. Indeed, both enjoyment and effort are characteristics of those *transitional* activities that link the fun and exuberance of childhood play with the structures and symbols of adult society.[19] Adults who take great pleasure in "surfing the net," cabinet making, or fly fishing, while taking their subjects seriously enough to read and practice them, demonstrate the ability to integrate the worlds of work and play. But learning to use leisure meaningfully in this sense is not likely to be the result of simple modeling or instruction. The ability to find enjoyment in intense involvement most likely derives from earlier patterns of play and self-directed activities and what they contribute to emotional and social development.

Emotional Development

A degree of emotional stability is necessary for effective social interaction. Without a modicum of trust and self-confidence, exploration and engagement with others is likely to be limited. Emotional stability is a mediating factor in the relationship between self-directed activities such as play and socialization.

The curative powers of play are evident in the earliest stages of life. Toward the end of the first year, children develop what Piaget called *object permanence*.[20] This is the understanding that people and things continue to exist somewhere even when out of the child's presence. The difficulty with this development is that it also brings an awareness that parents actually leave and go somewhere else; and, as a result, it is the source of separation anxiety that emerges so strongly at the same time. Most infants and toddlers find peekaboo a delightful game. Arousal is raised when big sister hides behind the chair, and the tension is dissipated with great relief and laughter when she appears with a resounding "peekaboo." Infants and toddlers are also fond of knocking things off their high chairs—much to the chagrin of parents—and then looking over the edge of the chair tray to see where the objects have gone. The fact that a parent picks up the object only reinforces its game quality, and it is often repeated ad infinitum. These patterns reflect the emotional value of play that makes it a resource throughout childhood.

Play is even used in therapy to enable children to deal with anxiety-producing and traumatic events.[21] Playing out anxieties—playing doctor shortly after receiving medical care, for example—gives a child a degree of mastery over the situation and enables him or her to assimilate the experience.[22]

Cultural differences in child rearing are also associated with the anxiety-reducing powers of play. In a now-classic study of fifty-six different native cultures, John Roberts and Brian Sutton-Smith found a relationship between a culture's particular emphasis in child rearing and the games that were preferred by the children in that culture.[23] In cultures where there was a great emphasis on obedience, children were likely to prefer games of strategy; whereas in cultures where child rearing was unpredictable, games of chance were preferred. The investigators' interpretation was that in at least some cultures games served the purpose of *assuagement* of the conflicts arising from the demands of adults in the society. If adults are overbearing, stress is released in games related to strategy; if they are unpredictable, the stress of not knowing is relieved in games of chance; and where high expectations create pressure, games of skill are preferred.

As children develop cognitively, they are increasingly able to accomplish through humor that which required acting out in play (in the roles of doctor, teacher, father, and so on). Making "light" of troubling events becomes both a cognitive and an emotional skill. In adolescence the frustrations and anxieties related to school and family interactions and expectations may be diffused in more casual sociability or in laughing and talking while hanging out with friends. The disengagement associated with these particular "faces" of leisure—the relaxed, casual one or the mirthful smiling one referred to in Chapter 1—gives leisure the same buffering effect that play provided in earlier periods, thus reducing the anxiety associated with troublesome social interaction.

If sharing with others has some value in "relativizing" the usual sources of stress, then being alone offers different advantages. Time alone generally evokes the experience of loneliness and depressed mood, as was noted in Chapter 3.[24] Being alone, especially to the extent that it is perceived to be an indication of rejection, is a painful condition for most adolescents and may undermine confidence. Adolescents are, in fact, more likely to link leisure with social interaction than with being alone.[25] Nevertheless, solitude has experience advantages that make it a precursor of a substantial part of adult leisure. Being alone affords time for personal assimilation and integration.[26] Solitude increases the likelihood of relaxation, rest, contemplation, and peacefulness. Such experiences are far less attractive in adolescence than they become in adulthood, but the discomfort most adolescents feel in being alone is often offset by the stabilizing that such experience provides. Certainly the choice one has in the matter is likely to determine the desirability and leisureliness of being alone; but evidence with adolescents indicates that moods and cognitive efficiency are better after periods of solitude than after periods of group interaction.[27] And those who learn to look at solitude as an opportunity rather than a curse are more likely to find this advantage in the leisure of adulthood.

Finally, though, to return to involvement in serious activities, the stress that children sometimes experience with high performance expectations might be expected to be emotionally maladaptive. Certainly, youth sports is often a target of criticism in this regard as adults put inordinate amounts of pressure on children to perform well. But research on stress in organized children's sports indicates that it is no higher for children than in other performance contexts such as music performances and classroom testing.[28] And the question of the loss of play and enjoyment notwithstanding, the stress that is endured in such contexts may even have an inoculation effect in making children and adolescents emotionally stronger and more resilient in other emotionally demanding situations. Still, negative effects are not uncommon for those who fail to reach the expectations of others, and failure in performance contexts can be particularly painful. Indeed, the highly structured and visible nature of such activities may make it impossible to escape that failure. Such conditions are linked with the *learned helplessness* syndrome (where one essentially gives up) that Martin Seligman found to be predictive of depression.[29] Obviously, the emotional costs of failure in performance contexts need further research attention.

Social Competence, Morality, and Relatedness

The ability to be at ease with people, to be effective and persuasive with them, to be responsive to them, to treat them fairly and to trust and love some of them are all important objectives of socialization. "Social competence" might be the best umbrella term, but moral development and a capacity for intimacy also come into play. These inclinations are intrinsically motivated to a great extent, deriving from the need for relatedness, and thus they are likely to be shaped further in the freedom of leisure. The fact that such social motives also benefit society makes them a priority for socialization as well.

Like emotional development, social development is influenced by play in early childhood. The play of parents with children contributes to the development of interaction skills and to the perception of others as sources of shared enjoyment. Children whose parents play actively and even physically with them in early childhood seem to get along better with their peers once they begin school.[30] And once children start playing games with peers, they develop an elaborate repertoire of social skills.

The games children organize for themselves in childhood provide a context for exercising social skills that will remain useful. In fact, Piaget, David Elkind, Janet Lever, and others[31] have suggested that games and sports are ideal contexts for learning organizational skills such as the ability to manage diversity of membership, adjudicate disputes, and work for collective goals. An argument over whether to increase the numbers on each team beyond the usual limit to accommodate newcomers or to exclude them from playing, for example, would test the social skills and moral reasoning of the players. Lever noted that such experiences are more common to the games boys play during this period than to those that girls play. Boys' games show greater role differentiation, interdependence, group size, explicitness of goals, number of rules, and team formation and coordination than do those of girls, thus conferring on the males an advantage in this kind of "training." And boys are more likely to work through disputes to keep the games going while girls more typically abandon the game if conflict arises. But Carol Gilligan[32] argued that it is just the fact that girls are less willing to sacrifice their friendships for "the good of the game" that defines their approach to life and relationships in contrast to that of boys. The girls' ethic of care makes a failed game expendable. Both of these orientations demonstrate social competence, though in different respects.

Given the influence of Title IX and other changes, the gender gap has narrowed substantially in the twenty-five years since Lever's studies. The more important point here, however, is the prospect that self-directed game playing contributes to the development of organizational competence or the ability to engage in collective self-regulation to achieve a set of shared objectives.

The ability to negotiate and reach agreements in games may have a significant impact on moral development as well. In discussing the importance of children's self-directed games for the development of social and moral competence, Elkind argued that

> children learn the other side of contracts with other children and with siblings. Here the relationship is one of mutuality; it is not unilateral. In playing and working with other children, young people can begin to expect such behaviors in return for certain favors. In childhood, the rewards for obeying contracts are most often personal acceptance. For example, a child that shows he or she is willing to abide by the rules of the game is permitted to play. It is with peers that children learn the reciprocal nature of contracts and how to be on the giving as well as the receiving end.[33]

Part of the social competence children develop through games likely involves a maturation in moral reasoning as well. Taking the perspective of others is necessary for the decentering that in turn allows for a progression in moral reasoning. The sequence was somewhat of a puzzle for Piaget, however:

> But is it the consciousness of autonomy that leads to the practical respect for the law, or does the respect for the law lead to the feeling of autonomy? These are simply two aspects of the same reality: when a rule ceases to be external to children and depends only on their free collective will, it becomes incorporated in the mind of each, and individual obedience is henceforth purely spontaneous. True, the difficulty reappears each time that the child, while still remaining faithful to the rule that favors him, is tempted to slur over some article of the law or some point of procedure that favors his opponent. But the peculiar function of co-operation is to lead the child to the practice of reciprocity, hence moral universality and generosity in his relation with his playmates.[34]

The contribution of play to social development may precede interaction in games, however. In Vygotsky's view, even in their earliest make-believe play, children are stretching through their "zone of proximal development" to understand social roles and social rules.[35]

Piaget believed that early childhood play is essentially immature, un-accommodated behavior and therefore of little adaptive social or intellectual value. But as Vygotsky argues, playing house or doctor does have rules and order. While accommodation to the external world is not overt, a sense of the rules and roles associated with the represented context is critical.

Even more important for our analysis, though, is Vygotsky's idea that a child learns in such play that voluntary obedience to self-chosen rules is required in the interest of achieving one's desires, and that individual satisfaction in socio-dramatic play with others can be enhanced by rudimentary cooperation. While such early preschool-age play may not require the perspective taking that accompanies the negotiation of games with rules in later childhood, it does give children experience in developing their own rule governed behavior. In such play are the seeds of the culture-building potential of leisure.

If the value of play and games to social development depends on the child's regulation of play events, it should not be surprising that adult direction of play activities is as controversial as it is. Children's games have become "youth sports," to a great extent, managed by coaches and organized by parents and league officials. And even though children are generally able to maintain their own subcultures in these arrangements,[36] they clearly do not benefit in the same ways when important decisions about the structure and direction of play have been taken out of their control.

Bringing children together in organized sport addresses a number of other developmental tasks, however, such as learning skills necessary for games, persevering in the face of obstacles, developing a sense of justice and fairness, and subordinating oneself for a greater good.[37] But the emphasis on performance and winning can undermine those purposes as well. Research by Harry Webb and others on children's orientations toward game playing demonstrated changes with age and grade in school.[38] Webb asked a group of children of different ages the question, "What do you think is most important in a game?" He had them rank "to play as well as you are able," "to beat your opponent," and "to play fairly." This research shows that as children get older and become more involved in organized sports, they are more likely to value beating an opponent than playing well or fairly. In a sense, Webb argued, children become *professionalized* in such games. The outcome becomes so important that it is more like work than play. Indeed, when adults are in control and place so much emphasis on competition and winning, perspective taking and empathy are largely unnecessary and may even impede performance. In an experimentally arranged "Kick Soccer World Series," a colleague and I found that the elementary-school children who were randomly selected to participate showed less generosity afterward than children who weren't selected to participate. And Shields and Bredemeier report data suggesting that continued involvement with major sports can be detrimental to moral reasoning.[39]

The positive contributions of sports activities to social development have less to do with character building than with learning to subordinate one's interests for the greater good of the team. It is no secret that the corporate world often recruits those with athletic experience because of their training in competitiveness, team loyalty, self-sacrifice, and commitment to collective interests. Still, such faith may not always be well placed. For one thing, the organizational effectiveness of a former athlete may be more attributable to pre-sport, child-directed game playing of the kind that Lever recognized as formative; much of the organizational behavior of athletic teams, after all, is controlled by coaches. Second, the competitiveness that someone brings to a corporate setting can be as destructive to intragroup relations as it is useful in securing market share.

The individualism associated with competitiveness can also be problematic for personal relationships. While loyalty to teammates and those who share the experience of an intense competition may be bonding, the inherently self-aggrandizing nature of sport makes it a poor training ground for the nurturance and sensitivity that is required for establishing intimate relationships. Intimacy comes more easily to females than males in any case, but it is especially difficult for those who have been fixated on competitive success as a source of self-esteem and identity or frustrated by the lack of that success. As women's sports expand and gain social status, there is some concern that they will also become as ruthlessly competitive as male sports. If this occurs, their ability to reinforce relational skills among women may be diminished.

Establishing an intimate relationship usually involves a willingness to modify one's own interests to accommodate those of another. Shaping mutuality in the development of a relationship requires some degree of vulnerability and flexibility, qualities that may be in short supply for individuals who have been very self-possessed and competitive in the course of adolescence. In the absence of such difficulties—or once they have been surmounted—the cultivation of shared enjoyment is likely to foster intimacy and deepen commitment.[40]

The social tasks of adolescence and early adulthood may benefit more from unstructured leisure contexts since there is more influence over communication and interaction patterns in those situations than when adults are in control. Adolescents in search of companionship and/or romance seek out such fourth-environment contexts as shopping malls, house parties, coffee shops, and swimming pools.[41] And even when activities are organized and structured for children by adults, informal child-centered interaction is likely to persist as part of the experience. Gary Alan Fine's perceptive studies of Little League baseball and similar activities have revealed vibrant *idiocultures* of shared language, meanings, and symbols that evolve in spite of the adults who direct the activities.[42] Children and adolescents in such situations help each other cope effectively with performance demands while still fostering a "team spirit." Fine and Mechling point out that "the experience of loyalty to the group through selfless rendering of service and even sacrifice for others amounts to a form of *moral education.*"[43]

The Development of Personal Competence

Accomplishing or producing something of worth and value to society, and being recognized for it, is also an important indication of socialization.[44] According to Erikson, this issue emerges in later childhood once a sense of initiative is established and standards of performance and comparison are provided. School is the most obvious venue for developing competence and reaching noteworthy levels of performance. But opportunities for competence development and achievement also come within the context of leisure.

Beyond the control of fears and the development of social skills, play also has a significant role in the shaping of self-confidence. The transformative qualities of play, while not productive in an immediate sense, contribute to inventiveness and flexibility, valued sources of creativity. Furthermore, the ability to improvise and expand one's world in play, as Vygotsky asserts, is also a source of self-confidence. By freeing thinking from the constraints of the external environment, play prepares the child with a degree of confidence to take responsibility for creating his or her world.[45]

As skills initiated in play are shaped and put to the test in the games and peer-oriented activities of later childhood (and later in more formal settings), competence grows. Competence develops not only in activity skills but also in problem-solving strategies and the ability to manage emotions and the social processes referred to earlier. Activities such as preparing for a camping trip that lead to immediate and specific feedback, that allow for social experimentation and self-testing, and that require planning and time management are addressing developmental tasks as well.

Of course, performance contexts in later childhood, as is true of school, can have a discouraging effect on interest. Social comparison focuses increasingly on outcomes in later childhood,[46] and failure to achieve—whether it be in a science fair, a pet show, or a swim meet—can be deflating to interest, enthusiasm, and self-esteem. But persistence in such activities in the face of limited ostensible achievement may foster resilience in other endeavors. Belief in this effect reinforces the investment of community leaders in organized leisure activities in childhood and adolescence. As a child moves into adolescence, schools provide these activities with the assumption that achievement in them will contribute to development more generally and will not interfere with academic achievement or may even enhance it. This assumption, which speaks also to the generalization of skills, has been the subject of a good deal of research.

Extracurricular Activity

The word *extracurricular* usually refers to activities that are done in conjunction with school while being supplemental and unnecessary to primary curricular activities. In fact, when extracurricular activities do have a clearer relationship with the curriculum, as with a computer club, they are often called "cocurricular."[47] But if the school's mission includes a broader view of development, such a distinction loses its importance; extracurricular activities serve a wide variety of school purposes. Nevertheless, most of the research on the influence of extracurricular activities (ECAs) focuses on academic orientations and achievement. And since academic development plays a large part in socialization for adult roles, that research is especially important.

There are at least five possible relationships between extracurricular activity and academic achievement: (1) the ECA is *directly supportive* of academic achievement—it nurtures skills that are transferable to the classroom setting or provides a context for the practical application of classroom skills; (2) the ECA is *compensatory and indirectly supportive* of academic achievement (through relaxation and restoration of energy); (3) the ECA *complements* academic achievement, serving other aspects of adolescent development—social problem solving, strategic planning and organizing, and leadership training, for example—that normal classroom activities are not able to address because of other more narrowly defined academic priorities; (4) the ECA is *disruptive* to academic achievement, interfering with success in academic work and/or other adolescent tasks; and (5) the ECA is *neutral* with respect to other aspects of adolescent life, having little or no influence, positive or negative.

To begin with the evidence available on ECAs and adolescent development, an integrative study in the *Review of Educational Research* [48] offers a relatively comprehensive accounting. This review of more than thirty studies revealed a mostly positive relationship between participation in ECAs and self-esteem, improved race relations, involvement in political and social activities in young adulthood, academic ability and performance (at least for males), educational aspirations and attainments, feelings of control over one's life, and lower delinquency rates. Although the review was too extensive to capture in its entirety here, Table 4.2 summarizes the relationships found.

Nonsport ECAs relate positively more consistently to the outcome variables than does athletic involvement. But design limitations hinder interpretation in any case. Most of the studies reviewed in this report were neither experimental nor longitudinal and therefore could not establish causality. The studies generally used limited convenience samples; they did not take into account moderator variables (IQ, parents' occupations, curriculum, previous grade-point average, race, school orientation, and school size); nor did they address such important factors as the duration, kind, and success of participation. Also they were typically atheoretical and generally failed to consider the mechanisms of influence. One-time observation studies are not designed to sort out questions of causality. An alternative explanation for many of the positive relationships is that participants self-select into such activities and are different from the start. Children with low self-esteem, for example, are likely to avoid performance contexts

TABLE 4.2

Number of Significant Relationships Found in Studies of Extracurricular Activities (ECAs) and Other Variables (1963–1992)

	Sports Participation Only			*Nonsport ECAs*		
	+	x	0	+	x	0
Academic success	5	4	5	4	–	–
Education aspirations	5	–	–	1	–	–
Education attainment	1	1	–	3	–	–
Self concept	1	2	1	–	–	–
Positive personal/ social characteristic	3	2	–	3	–	–
Negative social behavior	1	3	–	1	–	1

+ = positive relationship between participation and variable of interest
x = negative relationship between participation and variable of interest
0 = no relationship or mixed relationship

where their inadequacies are exposed. Longitudinal approaches are needed to demonstrate change as a function of participation.

Fortunately, there have been a couple of studies done fairly recently that have attempted to manage these limitations. Camp[49] used a national longitudinal data base of 7,668 seniors to examine the relationship between participation in student activities and achievement while controlling for measures of those variables at an earlier time. He found student activities to be a better predictor of subsequent academic achievement than study habits; and he argued further that the failure to find a negative relationship brings into question rules that exclude academically marginal students from participation in ECAs (e.g., the "2.0 [GPA] rule"). Thus, while there would still be ample reason to question policies of exclusion from ECAs on the basis of what other developmental values might be served for participants, such exclusion appears to be unwarranted even on academic grounds. In an elaborate regression analysis of a national ("High School and Beyond") data set, Marsh controlled for background variables and dependent-variable scores from several years earlier to show a modest but significant positive relationship between total ECA participation and self-concept, academic achievement, and educational aspirations, among other factors.[50] He concluded that there was less support for the "zero-sum" hypothesis—that ECAs subvert the time and attention that would otherwise go to course work—than for the idea that ECAs bring about some "commitment to school."

Another line of longitudinal research has addressed the impact of extracurricular activities over a longer period, predicting adjustment and well-being ten to twenty years later.[51] Modest positive relationships have been found suggesting an enduring impact of activity involvement in the years to follow. But alternative explanations, such as the mitigating influence of social class, cannot be ruled out.

An important question on the relationship between extracurricular activities and academic achievement is, For *whom* are such activities most important? Those who are very successful within existing academic circumstances may benefit from ECAs in diversifying their interests, in shaping their applied intelligence, and in learning to work with others in ways rarely afforded in classroom contexts. But there are many students whom schools fail to reach in any manner. Dropping out of school remains an important issue that relates to other social problems. And many who stay in school barely go through the motions, investing little of themselves in the curriculum. If attention, investment, and commitment are critical to success, schools must find noncoercive ways to cultivate those qualities in all students. ECAs might be a good place to look.

Still another problem with research on the subject is the fact that little attention has been given to the extent of involvement in particular activities, the role played, the success achieved, and the dynamics of the experience. Activities differ in their potential for enjoyment and development both in their inherent structure and in how they are practiced. Team sports, for example, require the coordination of one's attention with that of others in ways that individual activities, even individual sports, cannot; and the development of auditory discrimination occurs far more readily in music than in sports, while experience with student government may enhance organizational and problem-solving skills.

In sum, all the possible relationships identified at the start of this section might apply at different times. Depending on the circumstances, the people and activities involved, and how those activities are structured, ECAs can facilitate or impede other aspects of development, or they may simply offer a pleasant diversion. In any case, there are many for whom the question is moot; because such activities are conventional and normative (and, indeed, reproductive of many of the social patterns to be found elsewhere in society),[52] unconventional alternatives are more attractive.

Deviance and Conformity

When leisure is valorized as inherently positive, it is difficult to see it as maladaptive; but to the extent that discretionary time is used in the expression of deviant and delinquent behavior, and insofar as such behavior often brings a kind of enjoyment, leisure is definitely involved. In practice, leisure activity is often seen as a deterrent to delinquency, but the evidence for this is equivocal.[53] Free time itself has been found to be a "risk" factor, predisposing children and adolescents to delinquent and deviant behaviors.[54] And highly structured activities that are designed to keep children and adolescents off the street may become so unappealing that they pale in comparison to the attractions of the street.

Intensity of experience is a significant part of adolescence. Loud music, bright lights, and other extreme forms of stimulation have more appeal for adolescents than for any other age group. This appeal is partly a function of group identification and affiliation. Sharing in extremes of behavior confers a sense of belonging. And this often has the "deviation amplifying" effect referred to in Chapter 3;[55] gleefully indulged departures from the norms of society are more likely to meet with encouragement than reproach from peers. Experimentation with alcohol and other drugs is consistent with this tendency, although many other factors are involved. Alcohol use combined with aggressive and boisterous acts are part of masculine socialization in many societies,[56] while the use of psychoactive drugs is attractive as a means of enhancing awareness and vivifying sense perception.[57] Whatever the particular experience, sharing it with some, away from others, can be a superficial form of validation.

Correlation evidence on the relationship between delinquency and leisure activity lends modest support to the notion of activity engagement as deterrent. But, as was true of the research on the relationship between academic achievement and self-esteem, ensuing longitudinal research has been somewhat deflating, suggesting again a selection effect in most cases. Children and adolescents involved in delinquent activities are less likely to get involved in recreational activities and programs in the first place. In a cross-lagged panel study over five years, Reed Larson found that delinquency suppresses sports participation rather than the reverse.[58]

Given the relationship between free time and delinquent or criminal behavior, providing structured alternatives seems prudent. And public recreation has a growing mandate to address the problem in that manner. But are such programs any more than a temporary diversion? To offer more, activity experiences and outcomes of involvement must make subsequent deviant behavior less attractive by comparison. Larson's research indicates that in contrast with sports, arts and hobbies seem to be more effective in reducing delinquency. Perhaps they offer more in the way of useful, generalizable skills. Attracting delinquent adolescents to such programs is the biggest challenge in any case (and legal coercion creates a significant obstacle in generating intrinsic interest); adolescents in general are a difficult target group for public providers, since to participate amounts to a "pledge of conventionality"[59] that many, especially those who already feel themselves to be on the outside, are unwilling to make. And, indeed, in their acts of deviance—drug taking or other forms of illegal behavior—adolescents often express their resistance to a culture that they find oppressive. Even legitimate activities such as skateboarding and snowboarding can have an "alternative" character that sets them in opposition to the mainstream culture.

Of course, it would be a mistake to see total nonconformity in such patterns. Identifying with and behaving like all members of an out group is certainly conformist in its own right; and gang behavior relies upon such commitment, loyalty, and overt conformity. As with involvement in conventional extracurricular programs, deviant activities reproduce the existing culture, albeit from the outside. In Eckert's ethnographic study of "jocks" and "burnouts," those categories referred less to particular activities than to those who identified with *all* school extracurricular activities ("jocks") and those who identified with none ("burnouts").[60] The former are upwardly mobile and conventional while the latter identify more with the disenfranchised. The lack of attractiveness and effectiveness of structured programs, then, is less attributable to the activities and experiences themselves than to their larger cultural context. Deviant activities that take people away from such programs create attractive alternative venues for self-expression and relatedness for some.

Unequal Playing Fields

Even those who have voluntarily quit the system and are in trouble, however, can be reached in structured, organized activities under the right conditions.[61] Shirley Brice Heath, a developmental linguist and anthropologist, identified inner-city adolescents who were school dropouts but who were nonetheless "survivors" by virtue of their involvement in a variety of organized activities. She noted the value of coaches (in art and drama as well as sports) who helped the groups to establish goals and promoted planning, collaboration, and other high-level social skills as well as rarely taught cognitive skills such as hypothetical reasoning ("What would happen if we did . . . ?").[62] Similarly, adventure-based "challenge" recreation programs like Outward Bound are most effective over the long term when they incorporate self-reflective "processing" at the completion of programs to draw connections between what has been learned in the activity and real-world situations.[63]

A recent Carnegie Commission study of risk and nonschool hours forcefully establishes the value of structured activities in reducing and preventing many of the problems associated with neglect and disadvantaged conditions.[64] Such groups as Boy Scouts, Girl Scouts, Campfire Girls, and 4-H Clubs offer sanctuaries from troubled streets. But group association is only part of it; one of the commission's sources identified "high-yield leisure," consisting of constructive learning activities, as critically important to those who overcome risky conditions.[65] Other evidence linked involvement in community organizations to the development of such individual "assets" as social competence, problem-solving ability, autonomy, a sense of purpose, and hope.

Unfortunately, schools are often the problem rather than the solution. Many children experience "years of failure" and grow averse to schooling. Indeed, those who stand to gain the most from such programs are least likely to identify with students in the mainstream of school culture. Furthermore, many urban school environments are "war zones": knives, guns, drug trade, and extortion are common. Placing remedial, alternative activities in the schools may be of questionable value in such afflicted environments.

Once again, though, it is *how* rather than *where* activities are organized. Adolescents are likely to reject any organized activities directed and controlled by adults, as noted earlier.[66] Sometimes, if they have decision-making power and exercise some control over what they do and how they do it, adolescents—even those who are contemptuous of adult culture—actually seek adult structure. This tendency was demonstrated over and over in the situations Heath observed and is the basis of the Carnegie Commission recommendations.

Overaccommodation, Reproduction, and Resistance

Games, sports, and other organized activities are acculturating to those who participate. This function helps to maintain social order. But if a culture has social problems, these, too, are likely to be reproduced in its expressive forms. Cultures must continue to evolve to be healthy, and freedom of expression in breaking with tradition is often necessary to create that kind of development. The freedom of leisure affords the possibility of some degree of resistance to existing cultural patterns and the creation of others.[67]

Structured recreation is not likely to encourage much resistance or culture creation, however. Providing opportunities to invest in activity, to set goals and persevere, and to develop a sense of competence contributes to socialization but is not likely to spur departure from the status quo. The enormous entertainment value of sports, in particular, perpetuates a kind of other-directedness; the qualities of character that can profitably be displayed there are restricted to those with popular appeal such as endurance and emotional control. Experimentation and creative self-expression are not encouraged in such settings.

Overaccommodation in sport is less common in females than males, however, for whom participation is more of a cultural expectation. For females, mindless overinvestment is far less likely. When girls continue to participate in high-level sports, it is often a sign of *resistance* to social norms, since it is less expected and even discouraged in some cases.[68] The evolution of women's sports in recent years, with some legislative help (Title IX in the United States), has a culture-creating quality. Women are making a statement about the ability to be as invested in sport as men. Whether they will suffer some of the same limitations of the experience remains to be seen.

A similar pattern is evident in sports for those with physical disabilities, whose participation is a sign of resistance to the stigma of their condition. Those who participate are liberated by the experience and encouraged to resist and defy conventions and expectations in other respects.[69]

Overaccommodation can also have a narrowing effect. Optimal, flowlike experience does not ensure optimal investment. A wide range of developmental tasks need attention at all ages, and intense investment in activities may interfere with the completion of those tasks. Devotion to an activity means slighting other important tasks. Indeed, in two studies of college students, athletes demonstrated less ego maturity than nonathletes.[70] The tendency for coaches and athletic associations to care only about optimal performance and not about development is a common problem in elite sports in the United States, giving rise to charges that athletes are being exploited. Steve Brock and I reached a similar conclusion after several studies of former elite athletes who retired from sports, some as the result of an injury.[71] The narrowing of attention to achieving excellence in their sport left them, when it was all over, with the challenge of catching up with themselves and becoming new people.

Socialization into Adulthood

Socialization does not end as an adolescent finishes school, gets married, or finds a full-time job, though these role changes signal the end of adolescence and the beginning of adulthood. The challenge of becoming established as an adult is a priority for those in their twenties and thirties,[72] and leisure activities can facilitate this process. It may be expected, for example, that professional people in some fields will play golf or attend certain fund-raising social events or that other workers will share meals or drinks together. Leisure activity has also been found to be important to family cohesiveness.[73] And even well after careers have been established and children have been launched, leisure activities maintain familial, social, and community integration. At the same time, leisure can be a refuge from the pressures of socialization. These are themes to which we will return in later chapters.

Conclusion

Socialization is a process that changes with the times. As noted in Chapter 3, the values of child rearing have changed dramatically over the last sixty or seventy years, with a growing emphasis on freedom, independence, and self-expression. Self-socialization is more common now as a result, though it brings with it some vexing social problems. Growing up in this postmodern era—with reduced influence from traditional rules, roles, and restraints and diminished relationships in family, work group, and church or ethnic group contexts— leaves one simultaneously liberated and insecure. Media and commercial influences have become poor but ubiquitous replacements for traditional institutions. A glimmer of hope is suggested, however, in the cultivation of leisure activities that are both adequately challenging and personally expressive. These activities may continue to offer experiential prototypes for making the most of time, energy, and potential.[74] Furthermore, we need only look back to the culture-creating patterns of children at play, even in organized settings, to see a natural, intrinsically motivated tendency to use such situations to strengthen bonds with peers, families, and communities in enjoyable action and celebration.

The reality, though, is that the play of childhood that was bound up with intense action, exciting interaction, or flights of private imagination largely disappears by the time one reaches adolescence. Instead, play impulses in contemporary adolescence seem to bifurcate into extrinsically motivated, socially compromised organized activities like sports on one hand, and culturally disruptive patterns of deviant behavior on the other.[75] Most common, though, is for play impulses to disappear altogether in mind-numbing submission to mere stimulation in television watching.

If models of socialization that make play more meaningful and work more enjoyable and more self-directed[76] receive greater appreciation, the loss of differentiation of work and leisure may not be as unpleasant as Christopher Rojek and others suggest.[77] In such a future leisure may lose its importance as a separate space, merging more clearly with work as a source of meaning and enjoyment. Until then additional research on the influence of play and leisure experience in the development of personal and social competence may identify when and under what conditions it is most beneficial to socialization.

Notes

1. These arguments with respect to play and leisure are set out in the works of Johan Huizinga, *Homo Ludens* (Boston: Beacon Press, 1955), and Josef Pieper, *Leisure, the Basis of Culture* (New York: Pantheon, 1962), respectively, while Mihaly Csikszentmihalyi considers similar points in *The*

Evolving Self: A Psychology for a New Millennium (New York: Harper-Collins, 1993).

2. There is precedent for this approach in the writings of M. Brewster Smith (e.g., "Competence and Socialization," in J. A. Clausen, ed., *Socialization and Society* [Boston: Little, Brown, 1968]), David Elkind (*The Hurried Child* [Boston: Addison-Wesley, 1981]), and others.

3. For example, R. Havighurst, *Developmental Tasks and Education* (New York: David McKay, 1972); A. W. Chickering, *Education and Identity* (San Francisco: Jossey-Bass, 1969).

4. R. Lerner and N. Busch-Rossnagel, eds., *Individuals as Producers of Their Own Development* (New York: Academic Press, 1981); R. Oerter, "Developmental Tasks Through the Lifespan," in P. Baltes, L. Featherman, and R. Lerner, eds., *Lifespan Development and Behavior,* vol. 7 (Hillsdale, NJ: Lawrence Erlbaum Assoc., 1986).

5. D. I. McLeod, *Building Character in the American Boy: The Boy Scouts, YMCA, and Their Forerunners, 1870–1920* (Madison: University of Wisconsin Press, 1983); Pieper, *Leisure, the Basis of Culture.*

6. M. Csikszentmihalyi, "Leisure and Socialization," *Social Forces* 60 (1981): 332–340.

7. M. Csikszentmihalyi and R. Larson, *Being Adolescent* (New York: Basic Books, 1984); D. Kleiber, R. Larson, and M. Csikszentmihalyi, "The Experience of Leisure in Adolescence," *Journal of Leisure Research* 18 (1987): 165–176.

8. D. Kleiber, L. Caldwell, and S. Shaw, "Leisure Meanings in Adolescence," *Society and Leisure* 16 (1993): 99–104.

9. For numerous examples of the "overjustification effect," see M. Lepper and D. Greene, eds., *The Hidden Costs of Rewards* (New York: Wiley, 1978).

10. See L. Barnett, "Developmental Benefits of Play for Children," *Journal of Leisure Research* 22 (1990): 138–153; J. Bruner, A. Jolly, and K. Sylva, eds., *Play: Its Role in Development and Evolution* (New York: Basic Books, 1976); J. F. Christie and E. P. Johnson, "The Role of Play in Social-Intellectual Development," *Review of Educational Research* 53 (1983): 93–115; M. J. Ellis, *Why People Play* (Englewood Cliffs, NJ: Prentice-Hall, 1973); and K. H. Rubin, "Fantasy Play: Its Role in the Development of Social Skills and Social Cognition," in K. H. Rubin, ed., *Children's Play* (San Francisco: Jossey-Bass, 1980), for critical reviews.

11. A. Nicolopoulou, "Play, Cognitive Development, and the Social World: Piaget, Vygotsky, and Beyond," *Human Development* 36 (1993): 1–23; B. Sutton-Smith, "Play as Adaptive Potentiation," *Sportswissenschaft* 5 (1975): 103–118. See also B. Sutton-Smith, *The Ambiguity of Play* (Cambridge, MA: Harvard University Press, 1997).

12. Nicolopoulou, "Play, Cognitive Development, and the Social World."

13. For elaboration of this point see G. A. Fine, "Good Children and Dirty Play," *Play and Culture* 6 (1989): 43–56; B. Sutton-Smith and D. Kelly-Byrne, "The Idealization of Play," in P. K. Smith, ed., *Play in Animals and Humans* (New York: Blackwell, 1984); and R. Schechner, "Playing," *Play and Culture* 1 (1989): 3–19.

14. Schechner, "Playing."

15. E. Erikson, *Childhood and Society* (New York: Norton, 1963), 209–221.

16. H. Schwartzman, *Transformations: The Anthropology of Children's Play* (New York: Plenum Press, 1978).

17. R. Stebbins, *Amateurs, Professionals, and Serious Leisure* (Montreal: McGill-Queen's University Press, 1992).

18. E. Greenberger and L. Steinberg, *When Teenagers Work* (New York: Basic Books, 1986).

19. Csikszentmihalyi and Larson, *Being Adolescent.*

20. J. Piaget, *The Construction of Reality in the Child* (New York: Basic Books, 1954).

21. V. M. Axline, *Play Therapy* (New York: Ballantine, 1969); Erikson, *Childhood and Society,* 222–234.

22. L. Barnett and B. Storm, "Play, Pleasure, and Pain: The Reduction of Anxiety Through Play," *Leisure Sciences* 4 (1981): 161–175; L. Barnett, "Research Note: Young Children's Resolution of Distress Through Play," *Journal of Clinical Psychology and Psychiatry* 25 (1984): 477–483.

23. J. M. Roberts and B. Sutton-Smith, "Child Training and Game Involvement," *Ethnology* 1 (1962): 166–185.

24. Csikszentmihalyi and Larson, *Being Adolescent*; R. Larson, "Secrets in the Bedroom: Adolescents' Private Use of Media," *Journal of Youth and Adolescence* 24 (1995): 535–550.

25. Kleiber, Caldwell, and Shaw, "Leisure Meanings"; Csikszentmihalyi and Larson, *Being Adolescent.*

26. R. Larson, "The Solitary Side of Life: An Examination of the Time People Spend Alone from Childhood to Old Age," *Developmental Review* 10 (1990): 155–183.

27. Ibid.

28. T. K. Scanlon, "Social Evaluation and the Competition Process: A Developmental Perspective," in F. Small, R. Magill, and M. Ash, eds., *Children in Sport,* 3rd ed. (Champaign, IL: Human Kinetics, 1988).

29. M. E. Seligman, *Helplessness: On Depression, Development, and Death* (San Francisco: W. H. Freeman, 1975).

30. K. McDonald and R. D. Parke, "Parent-Child Physical Play: The Effects of Sex and Age on Children and Parents," *Sex Roles: A Journal of Research* 15 (1984): 367–378.

31. Elkind, *The Hurried Child;* E. Devereux, "Backyard Versus Little League Baseball: The Impoverishment of Children's Games," in D. Landers,

ed., *Social Problems in Sport* (Urbana, IL: University of Illinois Press, 1976); J. Lever, "Sex Differences in the Games Children Play," *Social Problems* 23 (1976): 478–487; J. Piaget, *Play, Dreams, and Imitation in Childhood* (New York: W. W. Norton, 1962).

32. C. Gilligan, *In a Different Voice* (Cambridge, MA: Harvard University Press, 1982).

33. Elkind, *The Hurried Child*, 133.

34. J. Piaget, *The Moral Judgment of the Child* (New York: The Free Press, 1965), 71.

35. L. S. Vygotsky, "Play and its Role in the Mental Development of the Child," in Bruner, Jolly, and Sylva, *Play: Its Role in Development and Evolution;* Nicolopoulou, "Play, Cognitive Development, and the Social World."

36. See especially G. A. Fine, *With the Boys: Little League Baseball and Preadolescent Culture* (Chicago: University of Chicago Press, 1987).

37. G. A. Fine and J. Mechling, "Child Saving and Children's Cultures at Century's End," in S. B Heath and M. W. McLaughlin, eds., *Identity and Inner City Youth* (New York: Columbia Teachers College Press, 1993); R. Larson and D. Kleiber, "Free-Time Activities as Factors in Adolescent Adjustment," in P. Tolan and B. Cohler, eds., *Handbook of Clinical Research and Practice with Adolescents* (New York: Wiley, 1992).

38. T. L. Maloney and B. M. Petrie, "Professionalization of Attitudes Toward Play Among Canadian School Pupils as a Function of Sex, Grade, and Athletic Participation," *Journal of Leisure Research* 4 (1972): 184–195; H. Webb, "Professionalization of Attitudes Toward Play Among Adolescents," in G. D. Kenyon, ed., *Sociology of Sport* (Chicago: The Athletic Institute, 1969), 161–187.

39. D. L. Shields and B. J. L. Bredemeier, *Character Development and Physical Activity* (Champaign, IL: Human Kinetics, 1995). It is somewhat surprising in light of this finding that Shields and Bredemeier contend that the morality expressed in sport contests is *bracketed* and situational and thus unlikely to be transferred to other situations.

40. M. Csikszentmihalyi, "Love and the Dynamics of Personal Growth," in K. S. Pope, ed., *On Love and Loving* (San Francisco: Jossey-Bass, 1980).

41. R. Silbereisen, K. Eyferth, and G. Rudinger, *Development as Action in Context: Problem Behavior and Normal Youth Development* (New York: Springer-Verlag, 1986).

42. Fine, *With the Boys*.

43. Ibid.; Fine and Mechling, "Child Saving and Children's Cultures," 130.

44. Smith, "Competence and Socialization."

45. Nicolopoulou, "Play, Cognitive Development, and the Social World."

46. J. L. Duda, "The Relationship Between Goal Perspectives, Persistence and Behavioral Intensity Among Male and Female Recreational Sports Participants," *Leisure Sciences* 10 (1988): 95–106.

47. P. Haensky, A. Lupkowski, and E. Eklind, "The Role of Extracurricular Activities in Education," *High School Sport* 69 (1986): 110–119.

48. A. Holland and T. Andre, "Participation in Extracurricular Activities in Secondary School: What Is Known, What Needs to Be Known?" *Review of Educational Research* 57 (1987): 437–466.

49. W. Camp, "Participation in Student Activities and Achievement: A Covariance Structural Analysis," *Journal of Educational Research* 83 (1990): 272–278.

50. H. Marsh, "Extracurricular Activities: Beneficial Extension of the Traditional Curriculum or Subversion of Academic Goals?" *Journal of Education Psychology* 84 (1992): 553–562.

51. M. Glancy, F. Willits, and P. Farrell, "Adolescent Activities and Adult Success and Happiness: Twenty-four Years Later," *Sociology and Social Research* 70 (1986): 242–250; H. Marsh, "Extracurricular Activities"; E. Spreitzer, "Does Participation in Interscholastic Athletics Affect Adult Development? A Longitudinal Analysis of an 18–24 Age Cohort," *Youth & Society* 25 (1994): 368–387.

52. See, for example, P. A. Adler and P. Adler, "Social Reproduction and the Corporate Other: The Institutionalization of Afterschool Activities," *The Sociological Quarterly* 35 (1994): 309–328; and D. Eder and S. Parker, "The Cultural Reproduction of Gender: The Effect of Extracurricular Activities on Peer-Group Culture," *Sociology of Education* 60 (1987): 200–213.

53. For reviews, see R. Larson, "Youth Organizations, Hobbies, and Sports as Developmental Contexts," in R. Silbereisen and E. Todt, eds., *Adolescence in Context: The Interplay of Family, School, Peers, and Work in Adjustment* (New York: Springer-Verlag, 1994); and D. W. Osgood, J. K. Wilson, P. M. O'Malley, J. G. Bachman, and L. D. Johnston, "Routine Activities and Individual Deviant Behavior," *American Sociological Review* 61 (1996): 635–655.

54. Osgood et al., "Routine Activities and Individual Deviant Behavior"; Carnegie Commission, *A Matter of Time: Risk and Opportunity in the Nonschool Hours* (New York: Carnegie Corporation, 1992).

55. Csikszentmihalyi and Larson, *Being Adolescent.*

56. T. Burns, "Getting Rowdy with the Boys," *Journal of Drug Issues* 10 (1980): 273–285.

57. J. S. Bruner, "Nature and Uses of Immaturity," *American Psychologist* 27 (1972): 687–708. Bruner offered a more nonsocial explanation for the rampant use of psychoactive drugs among college students in the late 1960s, calling it an "intravenous version of competence via intersubjectivity," where other alternatives for the establishment of competence were unavailable or unattractive.

58. Larson, "Youth Organizations, Hobbies, and Sports."

59. L. Hendry, *Growing Up and Going Out: Adolescents and Leisure* (Aberdeen, Scotland: University of Aberdeen Press, 1983).

60. P. Eckert, *Jocks and Burnouts: Social Categories and Identity in the High School* (New York: Teachers College Press, 1989).

61. Fine and Mechling, "Child Saving and Children's Cultures."

62. S. B. Heath and M. W. McLaughlin, eds., *Identity and Inner City Youth* (New York: Teachers College Press, 1993).

63. J. Hattie, H. W. Marsh, J. T. Neill, and G. E. Richards, "Adventure Education and Outward Bound: Out-of-Class Experiences That Make a Lasting Difference," *Review of Educational Research* 67 (1997): 43–87.

64. Carnegie Commission, *A Matter of Time.*

65. R. M. Clark, *Critical Factors in Why Disadvantaged Students Succeed or Fail in School* (New York: Academy for Educational Development, 1988).

66. See also K. Roberts, *Youth and Leisure* (London: George Allen & Unwin, 1985), for more on this point.

67. See especially M. Csikszentmihalyi, *The Evolving Self.*

68. See, for example, B. M. Wearing, "Beyond the Ideology of Motherhood: Leisure as Resistance" *Australian New Zealand Journal of Sociology* 26 (1990): 36–58; S. M. Shaw, D. A. Kleiber, and L. L. Caldwell, "Leisure and Identity Formation in Male and Female Adolescents: A Preliminary Examination," *Journal of Leisure Research* 27 (1995): 245–263; and V. Freysinger and D. Flannery, "Women's Leisure: Affiliation, Self-determination, Empowerment, and Resistance," *Society and Leisure* 15 (1992): 303–322.

69. T. Williams, "Disability Sport Socialization and Identity Construction," *Adapted Physical Activity Quarterly* 11 (1994): 14–31.

70. A. Petitpas, "Identity Foreclosure: A Unique Challenge," *Personnel and Guidance Journal* 56 (1978): 558–561; M. Malmisur, "Ego Development of a Sample of College Football Players," *Research Quarterly* 47 (1976): 14–153.

71. S. C. Brock and D. A. Kleiber, "Narrative in Medicine: The Stories of Elite College Athletes' Career Ending Injuries," *Qualitative Health Research* 4 (1994): 411–430; D. A. Kleiber and S. C. Brock, "The Effect of Career-Ending Injuries on the Subsequent Well-Being of Elite College Athletes," *Sociology of Sport Journal* 9 (1992): 70–75.

72. D. Levinson, C. Darrow, F. Klein, M. Levinson, and B. McKee, *Seasons of a Man's Life* (New York: Alfred Knopf, 1978); D. Levinson, *Seasons of a Woman's Life* (New York: Alfred Knopf, 1990); G. Sheehy, *Passages: Predictable Crises of Adult Life* (New York: E. P. Dutton, 1979).

73. D. K. Orthner and J. A. Mancini, "Benefits of Leisure for Family Bonding," in B. L. Driver, P. J. Brown, and G. L. Peterson, eds., *Benefits of Leisure* (State College, PA: Venture, 1991).

74. R. Stebbins, "Casual and Serious Leisure and Posttraditional Thought in the Information Age" (Keynote address to the World Leisure and Recreation Association, Fourth World Congress, Cardiff, Wales, July 1996).

75. D. A. Kleiber and G. C. Roberts, "High School Play: Putting It to Work in Organized Sport," in J. H. Block and N. R. King, eds., *School Play* (New York: Garland Publishing, 1987).

76. For example, Csikszentmihalyi, *The Evolving Self.*

77. C. Rojek, "De-differentiation and Leisure," *Society and Leisure* 16 (1993): 15–29.

5 Leisure Experience and the Formation of Identity

Leisure interests make for good conversation at social events, in the hallways of schools, and at places of business. They also give hints of personal style, personal preference, and even enduring relationships. But just how important are they to a person's deeper sense of self? The principal point of this chapter is that leisure interests and activities are far more important in identity formation than most of those who have studied self and identity have indicated. One need only recall the connection between intrinsic motivation and self-actualization established in Chapter 2 to see some of the possibilities. It is reasonable to expect that identifying one's interests and following them with enthusiasm would have an important place in both self-definition and self-development.

Identity is at least as much a social as a personal phenomenon, however. In the previous chapter we noted that socialization is normally facilitated through identification with others—family, peers, classmates, teams, countries, cities, and so on. Seeing oneself as a part of other groups contributes to a sense of place and belonging. And others provide in turn a compass for individual thought and action. These processes are important to identity formation as well; they help to determine who one is in relation to others. The challenge generally comes in reconciling such social alliances with the more personal and unique aspects of self. One forms an identity partly by defining oneself in contrast with—or even in opposition to—others. If the problem of socialization discussed in the previous chapter is predominantly about the induction and integration of people into society, the problem of identity formation is largely about differentiation from others. But as with the dialectics of socialization, that is only part of the story. Identity formation involves connecting and identifying with people at the same time that one's uniqueness is of compelling concern.

Research on identity has given the greatest attention to self-definition in the domains of work, family, and political, religious, and social ideology. With the exception of Waterman's work on personal expressiveness,[1] which we will consider again shortly, the actions people take for enjoyment have not been adequately considered in research on identity formation. And yet when identity research is done in an open-ended fashion, asking "Who am I?"-type questions, people of all ages, but especially adolescents, regularly refer to leisure interests in defining themselves.[2] The actions that people take in the context of relative freedom are especially reflective of tendencies to define uniqueness and identify with others. This chapter will address these possibilities.

Activity is not the only way in which leisure is relevant to identity formation, however. After considering the subject of identity and its developmental characteristics, we will address the value of solitude and disengagement for identity formation in leisure. The opportunity for contemplation and self-examination, for the wistful wanderings of imagination, is nearly as important to identity formation as being actively expressive. The discovery or creation of alternative "possible selves" depends on it.[3] Imagining oneself as a great actor, athlete, artist, politician, or even computer technician is a catalyst for becoming one.

Finally, we will consider the possibility that leisure is at times detrimental to identity formation. Antisocial experiments may extend the self into territory that makes hierarchical integration especially difficult, while taking one's leisure activity too seriously and specializing in it to the neglect of other abilities can have a narrowing effect that limits differentiation in other areas.[4] But before turning to the positive and negative effects of leisure experience on identity formation, the complexity of the subject of identity requires some unpacking.

Dimensions and Dialectics of Identity

Defining Identity

The most common understanding in both psychology and sociology is that identity is a "personal theory of self." But the two disciplines often part company at that point. Sociologists tend to see identity as a social construct and typically neglect individual uniqueness, while psychologists often miss the social and cultural construction of identity by assuming a core personality that will unfold naturally if not impaired in some way. Erik Erikson's writing has been an influential source for theory and research on identity especially among psychologists (though his considerable attention to social and cultural context is often ignored by them). He included in identity "a conscious sense of individual uniqueness, . . . an unconscious striving for continuity of experience, and . . . a solidarity with a group's ideals";[5] that demonstrates "both consistent sameness within oneself (selfsameness) and a persistent sharing of some kind of essential character with others."[6] And while this is a fair characterization of the *nature* of identity, its substance is a "multiplicity" of feelings, values, tastes, personal characteristics, beliefs, interests, social roles, and social group memberships to which a person is committed.[7]

Dimensions of Identity

Personal Versus Social Identity

Psychology and sociology may have different views of identity, but the combination of personal and social aspects is generally recognized in both camps.[8] Personal identity is a product of internal consistencies and inconsistencies with one's past, differences and similarities one has with others, and plans and goals for the future. A colleague shared a profile of one of his doctoral students that seems to illustrate some of these properties. The student insists that there was never anyone among her family and friends who saw her as even going to college, much less continuing on to do graduate work; but her desire to express aspects of herself that were not valued (or even acknowledged) by the others in her world spurred her along and gave her a basis for transforming the way she views herself. Here is a clear example of affirming uniqueness relative to others and independently imagining one's own future.

Social identity is derived from *identification* with others, whether one is an Asian American, a brick mason, a girl scout, or a senior citizen. Identities are embedded within groups, not in opposition to them: families (son, daughter, wife, cousin), neighborhoods (next-door neighbor, United Way volunteer), schools (teacher, student, clerk, custodian), and economic institutions (preferred customer, dealer, secretary), for example.[9] Group identity may also include former roles such as ex-wife or ex-athlete; and it may reflect *assigned* conditions such as physically disabled, heterosexual, or multiracial. But identifications must ultimately be recognized and accepted by the individual to be significant, and some social categories that could be used to describe someone may not be personally meaningful. Being a Capricorn or a resident of Crestview Heights, for example, may not be defining for a person. Like personal traits, social categories have to be "owned" personally and recognized socially to be part of one's social identity.

Coherence

While the multiplicity of personal and social elements might suggest separate selves, as in multiple personalities, one's characteristics are organized into a unitary self. Disparate elements in one's identity can be accommodated, at least until they come into conflict, but they must be integrated into a coherent whole to be a part of one's identity.[10] The coherence of identity is sometimes threatened by its complexity, however. Having asked adolescents to describe themselves, Susan Harter[11] reports the response of a fifteen-year-old who demonstrates the ambivalence of relating to parental values ("study!") and friends' values ("be popular!"), which in turn conflict with a boyfriend's values ("relax!"); the resulting conflict makes her feel "phony."

Salience

Domains of interest—political ideology, religious beliefs, vocations, and avocations, for example—vary in their *salience* both across individuals and for the same individual at different points in time. Sheldon Stryker argued that role identities are organized into a self-conception according to a hierarchy of salience.[12] The higher the salience, the more important is the role and the higher the probability that various situations will be seen as opportunities to perform those roles. For example, to a person for whom the role of scout leader is particularly salient, any social situation, regardless of the presence of children or other scout leaders, is likely to be seen as an opportunity to discuss scouting and scouts. Or a salient domain may vary in terms of the characteristics reflected at any given time (e.g., moving from flamboyant guitarist, seeking to distinguish his style, to patient teacher of classical techniques).

Authenticity

Aspects of identity may also feel more or less *authentic* to a person. Authenticity is conditioned in several ways: (1) by finding and responding to one's inner characteristics and potentials; (2) by behaving "naturally" as opposed to "unnaturally"; and (3) by establishing a level of comfort or "fit" with the immediate environment. Erikson associated core identity with "the real me," the sense of being deeply and intensively active and alive, "an invigorating sameness and continuity."[13]

Alan Waterman offers a similar view in his work on personal expressiveness.[14] Referring to Aristotle's idea of the "daimon," the evocative true nature of a person, he argues that activities are personally expressive when they bring an awareness of some characteristics of self that are uniquely individual potentialities, that prompt the feeling that "this is who I really am."

In Waterman's view, people default on their "true selves" when forced to by environmental demands (for survival), social pressures, pleasurable distractions, or lack of will. The total absence of personal expressiveness results in "identity pathologies" such as *diffusion*, where one is not seeking (such as being distracted by meaningless pleasures), and *disguise*, where chosen identity components are not congruent with eudaimonic potentials (being determined by external contingencies such as status and wealth).

In some contrast with Waterman, Ralph Turner associated authenticity more with being *comfortable* in social situations than with being aligned with one's unique potentials.[15] Like Waterman, Turner noted that situational identities are often negotiated bargains rather than reflections of commitment and authenticity and that people feel least like themselves in institutions such as school, church, or work. But for Turner, authenticity is restored largely with the lifting of expectations.

When Turner asked students to identify when and where they felt most truly themselves, the majority indicated that they felt that way when being with others in "casual and personal conversation, in a purposeless encounter without sexual overtones."[16] While the "true self" was also often associated with resisting institutional constraints, it is this "customary" everyday self that seems most comfortable and authentic to people, in Turner's view.

This customary self is effected largely through what Norman Denzin referred to as "self-lodging," or "translating features of one's own identity into the selves, memories and imaginations of others."[17] Denzin regarded self-lodging as a motive, since—in contrast to the need to present oneself in a certain way—it makes the self "unproblematic." People feel most authentic in contexts of relative freedom from external expectations, where companionable others allow them to relax and feel comfortable. Denzin noted that self-lodging is indicated by nicknames, dress, speech styles, and gestures that contribute to a sense of belonging. While such circumstances imply an identity that is at least temporarily stable and coherent, *dislodging* can also take place. Being spurned by a lover or fickle friends is unsettling to identity, making it problematic again. And thus the process of identity formation is likely to begin again and again. In fact, one's identity will evolve and change throughout the life span.

The ideas of Turner, Denzin, Waterman, and others demonstrate some of the dynamic tensions experienced in relation to identity. Just how these tensions are played out developmentally will determine patterns of self-expression. But there are at least indications at this point that self-expression is facilitated through attunement to personal capacities and supportive companions and that this attunement in turn benefits the formation of identity.

Dialectics of Identity Formation

Identity formation is motivated in some cases, then, by a search for authenticity, for one's true self, while at other times and for other people it is driven by the need for stability and being a more consistent and predictable member of society.[18] But whatever motivates the search for and formation of identity, the process itself follows some of the same dialectical patterns of development that were reviewed in previous chapters.

Identity formation is first of all *age related,* emerging in early adolescence in conjunction with the cognitive changes that allow for abstract thought. In Piaget's view, the transition from concrete to formal operations enables one to consider abstractions such as truth and beauty and to form hypotheses and theories, even a theory of oneself. The difficulty in the early stages—and herein lies the first part of the problem—is in shaping a theory that is both accurate and useful. Given that a sense of self is initially constructed almost entirely in response to the reactions of others, having a view that is stable is extremely unlikely because of the constant flow of new and contradictory information. Indeed, the ability to consider oneself from the viewpoint of others initially leads to the misconception that one is in fact the continuous subject of others' attention. This "imaginary audience"[19] is a source of the notoriously disconcerting self-consciousness of adolescence. Such self-consciousness is disruptive to both performance and enjoyment.

Age and experience promote differentiation of the self, allowing more understanding of and control over the sources of information that are used for self-definition. The example discussed earlier of the fifteen-year-old girl in conflict over how she should act with her parents, peers, and boyfriend demonstrates such differentiation (in spite of the challenge that it creates for coherence). But identity becomes more internally determined with age, giving increasing importance to traits, wishes, and emotions.[20]

Identity is constructed through both differentiation and integration. Identity itself is an indication that integration has taken place, that a coherent, unified sense of self has been formed out of disparate characteristics. But differentiation creates the characteristics to be organized in the first place. Creating and recognizing distinctions in experience is the basis of differentiation. Differentiation allows a view of self that is at once more precise and more abstract—as tolerant, kind, and sensitive, for example, rather than simply as a nice person. And information is used selectively to create a self-image that is as positive as possible.

Still, discrepancies in self-perception arise and create pressure and distress wherever a unified, coherent sense of self is sought.[21] Adolescents distinguish "false" from "true" selves insofar as they feel they have to impress others or accommodate to the demands of intolerant adults. The fifteen-year-old Harter interviewed complained, "I can only be my true self with my close friends," contrasting them to her parents, who still treat her "like a kid."[22]

Discrepancies caused by status and relationship conflicts in early and middle adolescence give way to those that come with role interpretation as one moves into adulthood. Assuming the role of parent, for example, requires both differentiation and integration.[23] A friend who recently became a first-time parent has resisted embracing the role in the way others do it. She struggles with wanting to be more than the role of mother suggests yet also tries to be successful within the role. She does what she can to avoid being categorized as a "typical mom" (e.g., dragging pictures of the child out of her purse at predictable points and letting conversations with other mothers digress into endless child comparisons); yet she has found herself working on her singing and storytelling with the child so that she can be a "good mom."

As the principal processes of identity formation, *identification* and *individuation* also operate dialectically. Marilyn Brewer points to a principle of *optimal distinctiveness* in describing how individuals identify with groups.[24] Being like others brings the sense of being part of a collective, but it is meaningful to identity only where that collective is distinguishable from others. The need to be connected with others is satisfied within groups, whereas the need to be distinctive is satisfied in intergroup comparison. For example, adolescents are often criticized for conforming so much, yet in identifying so closely with peers, they are usually distinguishing themselves from adults or from other peer groups.[25]

Individuation in identity formation generally centers on the establishment of distinctiveness; but this process is as likely to occur in relations with others as in separating from them, a point that is often neglected in research on identity. One's identity may be found and/or elaborated in relating to others in intimate ways. Ruthellen Josselson identifies ways in which individuation and relatedness come together, including physical *holding*, where one's family and/or friends literally embrace a person for his or her achievements and provide a context of safety for exploration; *passionate experience*, where an intimate other is both a source of intense new experience and feedback for self-definition; and *eye-to-eye validation*, where one becomes either real or false in another's eyes.[26] Each of those processes is a way of being with others that benefits rather than detracts from individuation.

Josselson credits Erikson with recognizing how finding and taking a place in relation to others is as much a matter of individuation as identification. In fact, some writers doubt that one brings much of a preformed self to a relationship, as if the relationship is a unit separate from the individual; they argue that one's sense of self is formed primarily through the process of being in relationships with others.[27]

Exploration and *commitment* also operate dynamically and dialectically in identity formation. Exploration has been referred to as "a pe-

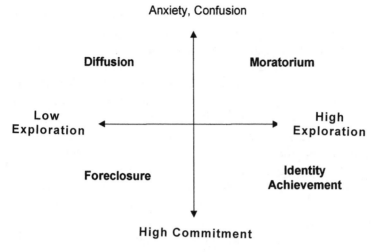

FIGURE 5.1
Identity Formation Statuses

riod of struggle or active questioning in arriving at identity decisions regarding goals, values, and beliefs," while commitment involves "the making of relatively firm choices regarding identity elements and engaging in significant activity directed toward the implementation of those choices."[28] The interaction of these processes results in four possibilities, according to James Marcia (see Figure 5.1). *Identity achievement* requires both exploration and commitment. Exploration in the absence of commitment—a common condition in adolescence—results in what Erikson and Marcia refer to as *moratorium*, a delay in the process of making decisions. Where commitments are made in the absence of exploration—often the result of simply internalizing values, beliefs, and wishes of parents—identity formation is at least temporarily *foreclosed*. And without either exploration or commitment, a person remains *diffused*, "uninvolved in the process of finding someone to be and sometimes even uninvolved in the process of finding something to do."[29] Identity achievement is the synthesis of exploration and commitment; moratorium represents exploration without commitment; and foreclosure reflects commitment without adequate exploration.[30]

These *statuses*, as Marcia calls them, apply to each domain a person experiences. As producers of their own development, people take steps—with some degree of freedom—to situate themselves in domains they find salient. Leisure affords some of the freedom necessary for exploration and in some cases for commitment as well.

A number of other questions come to mind at this point, however. When leisure is self-indulgent and digressive, does it reduce identification and threaten social integration? Conversely, when it is other-directed and accommodative, does it impede individuation? In allowing for experimentation with alternative selves, does leisure undermine coherence and integration? If leisure interests become salient and command commitment, do they then interfere with exploration and commitment in other domains? When, if ever, is the self-expression that leisure affords conducive to authenticity, to the identification and expression of unique potentialities of the kind described by Waterman? Alternatively, is leisure's contribution to authenticity primarily in allowing one to feel comfortable with others?

The Relevance of Leisure in Identity Formation

Social, institutional, and ideological commitments bring about the stabilization necessary for identity integration; but identity alternatives are often initially considered in the liberating context of leisure. Identity differentiation occurs both through experimentation with and elaboration of personal interests and through active identification with those who are apparently enjoying themselves. The decision to begin an activity may be based on little more than that appeal, but by sharing the activity with others a connection is formed. Identification with others is thus enforced in the sharing of patterns of action in an observable manner. Furthermore, adopting the language, dress, customs, and informal "codes of conduct" of other participants— whether it be in teams, clubs, computer groups, or even gangs—establishes membership in the group (to oneself and others) and may even affirm one's status as an "insider."

At the same time, leisure facilitates individuation in affording the opportunity for exploration of alternative ways of thinking and being. Leisure activities may be used to move apart from most of those who make up one's everyday social world. The imagination and creative experimentation necessary for individuation are often born in solitude and may benefit from the lack of evaluation by others. And yet others often recognize and reinforce the expression of special talents or idiosyncratic tastes. Furthermore, having others as validators of experience brings about some of the "comfort" that Turner associated with feelings of authenticity. Individuation and identification thus work dialectically in leisure to bring about identity formation. Experiences that are useful in the course of individuation need some social reference; and activities approached through group identification feel conformist without some semblance of individual differentiation.

Working Hypotheses

The dialectical processes of differentiation and integration, identification and individuation, and exploration and commitment suggest a number of specific propositions about the relationship between identity and leisure. As noted above, leisure can be a source of identification with others through even casual, superficial activities, but it contributes the most to identity formation when (1) it affords an opportunity for exploration of and experimentation with emerging interests; (2) the interests that emerge and are refined are truly personal and in keeping with other values; (3) action taken in response to interests creates feedback from the environment, including recognition from others, that reinforces the interests; (4) there is competence achieved in that action that defines and reinforces one's potentialities; (5) there is a degree of commitment to that action and to others who are involved; and (6) comfort with others emerges in the social world that is created around those interests and skills. The validity of each of these assertions will be examined in the rest of this chapter.

Leisure may also *constrain* identity formation, however, when (1) leisure choices are not linked effectively to other interests, talents, or commitments; (2) the commitment to an activity becomes so consuming that it limits attention to other potentialities; or (3) the actions taken meet with discouraging confirmation of negative aspects of self.

Sources of Interest

Two sources of interest are suggested in Waterman's discussion of the principal metaphors of identity formation.[31] The *discovery* metaphor posits an essential, authentic self to be revealed, whereas the *creation* metaphor suggests the self is only that which is derived through symbolic interaction with others and with the culture. Taken together, the metaphors are useful in describing the conflict between internal and external sources of information: self-definition is a lifelong developmental task that requires both discovery of one's own unique potentials and creation of oneself in response to opportunities. Waterman's view is that underlying potentialities are revealed primarily through self-discovery. Personal expressiveness then gives rise to emergent identity, and one's "daimon" is ultimately served.[32]

Both sources of interest are played out expressively in leisure; but it is primarily when they are refined through skill development and commitment that identity is most clearly affected. Initially, personal interests emerge from either of the two sources referred to above— appealing images that represent an attractive and ideal self or experimental actions that feel "right" and are revealing of individual potentials. The refinement of those interests, the development of skills related to them, and the commitment to social contexts where others share those skills are processes that follow from either beginning.

Discovery: From Experimentation to Interest

Initial action in leisure contexts may be tentative or extravagant depending on such individual differences as extroversion, openness to experience, and shyness.[33] Personality has more influence in leisure than in institutional contexts, such as school and work. This is not to suggest that leisure contexts are free of external determination; family leisure in particular reflects the roles and relationships of family life more generally, and all leisure experience is socially embedded in some way. But the opportunity to be more freely self-expressive and experimental is by definition greater in the context of leisure.[34] Playing and "fooling around" arise from curiosity and freedom, and interests emerge from such experiences.[35] Such behavior is not likely to result in the kind of feedback that contributes in any substantive way to one's sense of self, however, other than as a reminder that being a "player" is acceptable and even liberating. And yet as the particular actions, however experimental, become recognized as one's own, as they are experienced as personally expressive and as offering directions for cultivation of talent and association with others, the interests begin to reveal pathways to the self.

Play, then, has an important but limited role in identity formation; its impact is restricted to revealing alternative possibilities of being. Realizing the full value of those possibilities requires more. The experimentalism of play—free as it is from the need to bend to social convention or even one's past behavior—is consistent with exploration of alternative interests, roles, action patterns, modes of expression, and the like. "Trying on hats" is an apt metaphor here. In play no person or thing is taken completely seriously, so all is possible. The risks are limited, so play thrives on adventurousness; the more outrageous the better. Play brings about some of the differentiation that is necessary for individuation. But where the question of "how one looks when the hat is on" becomes an earnest one, the play is likely to be over—the play frame is broken, as Gregory Bateson would say,[36] and the question of identity is at issue. Hence play's limited impact: while it promotes the discovery of elements constitutive of identity, it does little to integrate them with other purposes of the self.

Creation: From Image to Interest

Exploration of alternative ways of thinking and being need not be overtly active, however. As Rollo May suggests, the opportunity to "pause" allows for the reflection necessary to consider possible selves.[37] Imagining ideal selves or even considering negative alternatives may be as important to the construction of identity as taking action and receiving feedback from the environment. The adolescents studied in Reed Larson's experience sampling investigations gave numerous indications that their experiences of being alone, while not always associated with positive affect, were important to their well-being and to their imaging of possible selves.[38]

People involved in enjoyable activities provide "identity images" and defining attributes for adolescents and others in a position to consider alternative selves. Thus, kayakers are regarded as being adventurous, independent, and outdoorsy, while guitarists are seen as easygoing, creative, and introspective.[39] These "prototypical attributes" are then cultivated as self-images in beginning participation; to the extent that such qualities are shaped by and/or give expression to one's existing qualities, a degree of self-affirmation takes place. Of course, in some cases individuals cultivate identity images without actually participating—by wearing the clothing of participants or frequenting the same locations, for example. Lois Haggard and Dan Williams give the examples of "gearheads" who wear high-tech equipment around hiking venues or "lodgesitters" who hang around in ski lodges but don't ski.[40] This kind of self-presentation and self-affirmation in leisure contexts, where there is a "sign value" to what one does and how one looks, is responsible for a great deal of consumerism[41] and represents a target of critics of the commodification of leisure, both past and present.[42] There is indeed a question of whether such crass posturing might even undermine the sense of authenticity if it hides a "true self." But identity images may be important in the stimulation of initial interest in activity in any case, and clearly they have a reinforcing effect as well.

From Interest to Skill

Learning to ride a bicycle in childhood may be initially appealing to six-year-old Luisa because the older girl next door is doing it, but it takes on a life of its own when it extends her range of enterprise and makes other bike riders part of an accessible reference group. The development of skills is an important part of the role leisure plays in identity formation. Participation in leisure activities apparently needs to be done relatively well to lead to the enhancement of self-concept; just doing an activity may not be enough to change a view of oneself.[43] This is also consistent with the flow theory of Csikszentmihalyi referred to earlier.[44] As a task, activity, or set of activities is mastered, greater difficulty and complexity is required to maintain interest, attention, and enjoyment, or flow. Mastering this added difficulty leads, in turn, to a growing complexity of the self, which contributes directly to the structure of identity.

The continuing contribution of skill development to identity also depends on the context of the activity, however. Emerging interest can be discouraged by conditions that prohibit or limit active self-expression. A budding interest in painting, for example, might be extinguished for lack of appropriate nurturance or opportunity. But in some cases such constraints only deepen commitment, and the efforts extended in overcoming them become part of the challenge against which one's abilities are measured and tested. Overcoming early failure in reaching a level of competence and learning to manage emotions is equally important in integrating a skill into a sense of self.[45] Pushing through constraints to take action that is intrinsically satisfying creates an "order in consciousness," as Csikszentmihalyi puts it,[46] that contributes both to a sense of competence and to an incorporation of that action pattern into one's identity.

From Skill to Commitment

As we have previously noted, the research and writing on identity formation has emphasized work, religion, sex roles, and political ideology. It is around these matters that values and beliefs are typically articulated. And Erikson was no exception in this regard, discussing vocational interests, political and religious ideology, and gender identification as the central elements of identity formation.[47] But he also noted that *favored capacities* have a constituent role in the evolution of identity,[48] and these are at least as likely to be explored, expressed, and developed in leisure as in other contexts.

The abilities shaped in games and sports become the favored capacities of some children and adolescents, but their significance for identity formation may be short-lived or limited only to the recreational domain.[49] In other cases, however, favored capacities in music, art, acting, singing, hobbies, adventuring, and so on, while embraced as play initially, come to carry some weight in a person's emerging personal and social identity. When such activities are taken seriously enough to submit to a discipline of training and application, they offer patterns of commitment comparable to those in work, church, and school. As Stebbins notes, serious collectors, musicians, and amateur astronomers show great perseverance and commitment and make sacrifices in time, money, and social relationships to serve their passions.[50] These activities are important in expressing individual talents and capacities, providing a degree of social recognition, and affirming central values and interests.[51] Intensely involving activities can be digressive or even regressive, of course; consider, for example, the surfer who only works long enough to collect unemployment insurance so he can devote all his time to surfing. But when such activities reflect continuity as well as complexification of the self through the expansion of competence *and* integration within the wider world, they are likely to be important in the course of identity development. A study of participation in juvenile jazz bands among girls in Scotland demonstrated that such experience can enhance both self-definition and social integration.[52] Playing together utilized friendship to foster a more disciplined approach to the activity and helped participants develop a sense of pride and commitment.

The jazz-band example points again to the importance of social context in identity formation. Identification with others in a music group such as this, having a name and perhaps even uniforms, is part of the initial embedding of identity for many children and adolescents, as Fine demonstrated in his study of Little League baseball.[53] Paradoxically, it is the subordination of self that seems to contribute the most to the identification. Around my town there is a popular T-shirt, originally worn by local athletic teams, that shows "TEAM" in large capital letters with "me" in lower case letters, of about one-third the size, below it. The point is to remind players that they must subordinate their "egos" for the good of the team. A commitment to team performance and success requires this relationship. At first glance one might see this as another example of the authoritarian coaching and doctrinaire training typical of sports; but Fine's notes on the tendency to sacrifice one's own interests for the good of teammates in competitors as young as nine—even *in spite of* the directions of coaches—suggests that the primary commitment is often to the peer group alone.

The connectedness that such identification and commitment creates is also stabilizing to identity in some respects. Coparticipants whose bond is based on shared activity become more accepting of one another, allowing everyone to be themselves. As Turner and Denzin suggested, the self-lodging that takes place after a time with close friends and companions leads to an ebbing of identity questions and an emergence of feelings of authenticity.

Comfort, however, may apply only to one's place with others in the group. The activity itself may continue to challenge one's comfort zones, especially where there is a significant outcome (a finished product, audience approval, victory, and so on) or compelling demands in the activity itself. Despite the fact that extrinsic rewards are generally outweighed by intrinsic motivation, much may be at stake in serious leisure activities. And the task absorption and worklike intensity of some activities are often associated with rather sobering risk, as in the case of rock climbing. Furthermore, the sense of obligation to the others involved puts the relationships at risk as well if the unwritten contract of commitment is violated.

Serious leisure activities, then, add commitment and social integration to what may have started merely as differentiating play. When an interest emerges, the cultivation of that interest in a way that is meaningful and important to one's identity typically depends on the development of greater levels of competence and on support from significant others. Such conditions usually result in the elaboration of the activity and the complexification of self. In this sense both differentiation and integration take place.

From Commitment to Commitment: Generalization of Effects

The lack of attention to leisure activities in identity research may reflect not only underappreciation of the significance of leisure but also a view that, however important leisure experiences may be, they have little to do with those domains of greatest importance to society: vocations, politics, and religion, among others. But this raises the question of whether identity formation in one domain has any impact on identity formation in other domains or some core sense of identity in general. If a young women has broken away from her parents' religious traditions, has explored a variety of other religious practices and orientations, and has committed herself to practicing within a religious framework of her own choosing, does this affect other aspects of her identity as well? And, because religious matters were of such salience to her, does this commitment have a stabilizing influence in its own right, regardless of where she is in other areas of life? Similarly, what is the impact on overall identity formation of, say, achieving success in learning a musical instrument and performing for others?

Although there is little empirical evidence on these questions, there are some indications of a *gradient* of potential influence in areas where there is some overlap—for example, in ideological and religious domains for the woman described above.[54] Experience with leisure and recreation may also overlap to some extent with one's self-perceptions in social and organization skills. In helping to arrange a 4-H crafts festival with fellow club members, a young man shapes organizational skills that enhance his awareness of vocational possibilities even though the primary impact of his involvement is in the area of avocational identity.

The effects of leisure experience on identity formation may depend less on the overlap of domains, however, than on the power of commitment to serve as a model for similar work in any domain. The sense of oneself as being capable of sustained effort and perseverance and as being able to derive enjoyment and social solidarity from personal investment in activities with others is a foundation for exploration of and commitment to other areas as well. The "transitional" quality of such activities is especially noticeable in adolescence, but it likely applies throughout the life span.

Transitional effects can be *facilitated* through intervention. Somewhat paradoxically, unself-conscious flow experience contributes to the growth of self only through the self-awareness that comes in retrospect through the realization of the growing complexity of self that has taken place as a result of the experience. That this process might be mediated in some ways has occurred to those who have tried to use activities therapeutically and developmentally. As we noted in Chapter 4, a debriefing or *processing* period immediately after such activities enhances the prospect that the changes in self-image can be generalized to other situations and domains.[55]

Such steps may be especially important with groups for whom other aspects of identity are psychologically or socially problematic. For a person with some limiting or stigmatizing characteristic, such as a physical disability, an identity-shaping preoccupation may provide significant compensation. Since body image is especially important in the early stages of identity formation,[56] a "failed body" becomes significant to psychological as well as physical development. The archaic term "invalid" makes the point most clearly when used to refer to someone who is physically disabled; developing physical skill and talents in music, the arts, and even sports may provide some redress for the social liabilities of such conditions.[57]

Leisure thus affords opportunities for the exploration of interests and for action and self-development that may be more self-affirming than those provided in more socially constrained circumstances. And the opportunity to play across the life span is especially important because play is the active, creative interpretation of values and abilities and an essential act of individuation. Nevertheless, patterns of identification in leisure activities and experiences in adolescence may be such that little of long-term personal value is derived. In some cases activities interfere with identity formation. Let us turn, then, to further specification of these possibilities and a closer examination of relevant research.

The Derailment of Identity Formation in Leisure

Deviance

The experimentalism of play is evident in drug and alcohol use and other forms of deviant behavior as well as in more socially acceptable activities. Drug use is clearly differentiating and, in spite of being disorienting, may contribute to a *sense* of creativity and self-expression. Indeed, such activity may come to replace other forms of experimentation that are more trustworthy in their formative potential. The costs of intoxication may be no greater than those from other forms of deviant behavior; but where one uses it to generate new images of self, begins to accept it as a regular pattern, and identifies with others who share the pattern, a kind of pseudocommitment exists that can become developmentally destructive.

With any form of intentionally deviant behavior, collaboration with others often reinforces a sense of independence and differentiation. This form of fun and experimental social interaction also triggers important changes for an adolescent who has been overly accommodating and unexpressive.[58] In addition, as was noted in the previous chapter, the reactions of adolescent peer groups are often "amplifying" to deviant activity as one becomes the "class clown," a "rebel without a cause," and so on.[59] Erikson refers to this as the "I dare you" version of social play, a "leaning out over precipices" that adolescents do as a kind of "semi-deliberate role experimentation" that shouldn't be taken too seriously by adults.[60] But again, there are only limited possibilities for integrating these behaviors with other aspects of self that are more consistent with meeting developmental tasks.

When deviant and delinquent activities become more involving, however, it is their similarity to serious leisure rather than their playfulness that deserves some attention. A wide variety of motivations contribute to delinquent activity, but for some it is the challenge that is most attractive. Delinquent behavior can be as "flow-producing" as other more legitimate activities, and it is also as likely to be as self-defining. Gang activity frequently brings with it commitment to patterns of action, a unique ethos, identification with the group, and effort and perseverance in the face of obstacles—qualities that are associated with serious leisure. There are numerous examples of delinquent activity that show the high competence-to-challenge match associated with flow experience.[61] Motorcyling teenagers in Japan have also revealed this pattern. *Bosozoku*, as it is called, engages participants in street races in which part of the excitement and the challenge comes in eluding police and in being seen as a law-breaking group.[62] But the "career contingencies" of delinquent behavior frequently involve turning it away from such playfulness and toward rather strictly instrumental, indeed criminal, incentives. When this occurs, the delinquency can no longer be compared with the serious leisure of amateurs and hobbyists.

Overinvestment

As noted in the previous chapter, if the experimentalism of exploring different roles and interests, the trying on of different hats, isn't tempered with some degree of commitment for a period of time, it is unlikely to have an enduring effect on identity. Conversely, identity formation may be limited by overcommitment, where the conformity associated with identification is so pervasive that it is de-individuating and one's sense of uniqueness is undermined all together. Such might be the case for the "real fan" who is devoted to an athletic team and lives for each subsequent event.

Strong identification with activities can *impair* identity formation in other ways as well. Being an athlete, and little else, may foreclose identity formation when there is little time for or interest in other domains. In such cases, considerable personal transformation is subsequently required.[63] And the same is theoretically possible with other activities to which one becomes "addicted" or even overcommitted, such as with music, surfing the Internet, and so on.

The negative impact of such intense involvement is likely to be mitigated by some of the factors that were reviewed earlier. First, to the extent that the activity is socially integrative, it will be less limiting than more socially isolated activities. Second, activities that are more clearly connected to one's unique potentials, to a sense of one's "daimon," in Waterman's terms, are likely to be more personally significant in other respects. Third, even if one's competence continues to be elaborated rather exclusively within a particular domain, the self is still being complexified to some extent. And finally, the applicability of one's skills to other domains can be actively addressed in the course of education and counseling.

Other-Directedness

Leisure activities that are wholly inconsistent with one's individual potentials can still be attractive if they have social-status value. Although enduring interests are often generated from appealing identity images, as was noted earlier, if they are only cultivated for their sign value and are not reinforced with some degree of personal development, they are unlikely to contribute to a sense of identity and may have the effect of obscuring alternative action patterns that are more personally meaningful. This is the "false consciousness" that comes with the commodification of leisure experience. Taste is clearly market driven and electronically mediated by television to a great extent, and many of the more powerful images are of physically attractive individuals enjoying active recreation. One need only study truck, jeep, and van television commercials to see the evidence.

Second, participating unsuccessfully in activities for which there are cultural expectations may be undermining to self-esteem and thus limiting to self-elaboration and development derived through differentiation. Failing at developing musical talent in a family of musicians, for example, could leave one adrift, at least for a while. Although persistence and effort may be particularly important in dealing with the lack of initial success in a given activity, self-esteem and self-definition may be undermined if some degree of success doesn't follow. Persistence out of responsibility to others rather than personal interest is likely to be more of a cost than a benefit to identity formation.

Leisure Identity and Stabilization

Identity formation occurs throughout the life span, but in adulthood there is far more stability than change in personality. Continuity becomes more important with age and is a source of security and integrity in later life. Leisure activity coincides with this pattern as was discussed in Chapter 3. Preference for novelty and variety in leisure activities gives way to some extent to those experiences that are as familiar as the friends and family members that share in the experience.

But life offers most people a variety of twists and turns that cannot be anticipated, and these events often create such a serious disruption in one's life story that personal change is inevitable. Leisure activities, especially those that involve serious commitment and the development of competence, often remain salient to one's self-conception in spite of such changes. Indeed, a reliance on leisure-related identities may serve as a buffer in dealing with significant and traumatic life events,[64] as will be considered in the next chapter. In such cases, when familiar activities are maintained, leisure experiences are a source of stability.

In some cases it is the lack of fit with an oppressive culture, rather than a disturbing event, that is personally destabilizing. Characteristics that define one as categorically different from the norm, as in the case of a physical disability referred to earlier, can be stigmatizing in a way that inhibits self-expression. Participating in wheelchair sports serves as a model of resistance to the oppressive effects of such a stigma. More common among the disenfranchised, however, is the tendency to retreat into more private forms of self-expression for stabilization and adjustment. For example, a study of gay and lesbian adolescents demonstrated that personal expressiveness was inhibited in public contexts where heterosexuality is assumed. In contrast, private contexts held special importance for allowing the respondents in the study to be more freely themselves.[65]

Conclusion

One of the leading writers on the psychology of self and identity, Roy Baumeister, pointed out that many traditional sources of identity have been trivialized, destabilized, or altogether lost. Religion, marriage, vocation, gender, geographical home, and ancestral family, among others, no longer have the defining effect on individuals that they once did. They have been replaced, he argued, by individual personality, personal accomplishment, personal style and interest, and *leisure* as contemporary sources of identity. About the last he says:

> The spread of leisure time to all levels of society has enabled people to take part in a wide variety of activities, and these hobbies and memberships help define the self. One is not just a clerk, one is a jogger and a guitarist as well as a clerk. Although most of the activities are done by many others, they provide a kind of local differentiation because there are so many possible combinations that one's own combination seems unique among one's acquaintances. . . . With the other joggers, one is the guitar player; among musicians, one is the clerk (with the "daytime job"); at work, one is known as the jogger or the guitarist.[66]

The perspective of postmodernism should be considered again here, however, especially with regard to those who do not develop serious leisure commitments. With the diminishment of influence of work, religion, and other social structures, the march of market capitalism and media technology leaves people with a kind of *multiphrenia*,[67] a vast number of possible selves challenging any semblance of unity and authenticity. The "formation" of an authentic self may be largely an illusion to the extent that it is shaped by media images and consumer choices. The sense of autonomy that an abundance of possibilities affords is at best a temporary hedge against the anxiety and confusion that follow from the complex conditions of contemporary life in Western cultures. Self-direction in this sense becomes merely *self-fashioning*.[68] Where there is little in the way of enduring personal characteristics and potentialities in which to ground the experimentally created self, integration becomes extremely difficult. An awareness of one's personal expressive history may be the best fortification against such dis-integration.

Movement through adolescence brings an accumulation of experience in home, school, peer culture, and society. As one's personal history provides elements that are integrated into a coherent sense of self, identity takes on the character of a "life story." The life story, which evolves throughout adulthood, has the power to tie together past, present, and future.[69] Novelist Barbara Kingsolver offers an illustration of how a leisure-based identity can be integrated into a life story:

> For all the years I've worked as a writer, I've played at keyboards and the odd wind instrument, and lately even conga drums. I have sung in the shower. (I sound *great* in the shower.) I have howled back-up to Annie Lenox and Randy Travis and Rory Block in my car. I've played in garage bands and jammed informally with musician friends, and with them have even written and recorded a few original songs. But I've *never* called myself a musician. It's not the one thing I do best.
>
> As I get comfortable with the middle stretch of my life, though, it's occurred to me that this is the only one I'm going to get. I'd better open the closet door and invite my other selves to the table, even if it looks undignified or flaky. Possibly this is what's regarded as midlife crisis, but I'm not looking for a new me, just owning up to all the old ones. I *like* playing music. The music I play has not so far been nominated as a significant contribution to our planet, but it's fun.[70]

The things we tell ourselves about who we are and what we do not only describe the self, they also serve in the creation of that self. It is a story that specifies a personalized "niche" in the adult world and so a sense of continuity and sameness. The story is the more complete answer to the questions, "Who am I?" and "How do I fit into an adult world?" Identity is, in fact, a life story. The relevance of leisure in "rewriting" one's life story following life transitions will be the focus of Chapter 6. Suffice it to say here, though, that revising one's life story in response to life events calls again for exploration and commitment and also for the resource of leisure.

Notes

1. A. S. Waterman, "Personal Expressiveness: Philosophical and Psychological Foundations," *Journal of Mind and Behavior* 11 (1990): 47–74; A. S. Waterman, "Two Conceptions of Happiness: Contrasts of Personal Expressiveness (Eudaimonia) and Hedonic Enjoyment," *Journal of Personality and Social Psychology* 64 (1993): 678–691; A. S. Waterman, "Finding Something to Do or Someone to Be: A Eudaimonist Perspective on Identity Formation," in J. Kroger, ed., *Discussions on Ego Identity* (Hillsdale, NJ: Lawrence Erlbaum, 1993).

2. G. R. Adams (personal communication, 1996); B. Shamir, "Some Correlates of Leisure Identity Salience," *Journal of Leisure Research* 24 (1992): 301–323; R. H. Turner, "Articulating Self and Social Structure," in K. Yardley and T. Honess, eds., *Self and Identity: Psychological Perspectives* (New York: Wiley, 1987).

3. See, for example, R. Larson, "Secrets in the Bedroom: Adolescents' Private Use of Media," *Journal of Youth and Adolescence* 24 (1995): 535–550.

4. R. F. Baumeister, *Identity: Cultural Change and the Struggle for Self* (New York: Oxford University Press, 1986).

5. E. Erikson, *Identity: Youth and Crisis* (New York: Norton, 1968), 208.

6. E. Erikson, *Identity and the Life Cycle* (New York: Norton, 1980), 102.

7. See, for example, S. Harter, "Self and Identity Development," in S. S. Feldman and G. R. Elliott, eds., *At the Threshold: The Developing Adolescent* (Cambridge, MA: Harvard University Press, 1990); and S. Rosenberg and M. A. Gara, "The Multiplicity of Personal Identity," in P. Shaver, ed., *Self, Situations, and Social Behavior: Review of Personality and Social Psychology,* vol. 6 (Beverly Hills, CA: Sage, 1985).

8. For a review of this point, see K. Deaux, "Personalizing Identity and Socializing the Self," in G. M. Breakwell, ed., *Social Psychology of Identity and the Self Concept* (London: Surrey University Press, 1992).

9. S. B. Heath and M. W. McLaughlin, eds., *Identity and Inner City Youth* (New York: Teachers College Press, 1993).

10. R. F. Baumeister, "Self and Identity: An Introduction," in A. Tesser, ed., *Advanced Social Psychology* (New York: McGraw-Hill, 1995).

11. Harter, "Self and Identity Development."

12. S. Stryker, "Identity Theory: Development and Extensions," in L. Yardley and T. Honess, eds., *Self and Identity* (New York: Wiley, 1987).

13. Erikson, *Identity: Youth and Crisis,* 19.

14. Waterman, "Personal Expressiveness."

15. R. H. Turner, "The Role and the Person," *American Journal of Sociology* 84 (1978): 1–23; Turner, "Articulating Self and Social Structure," in K. Yardley and T. Honess, eds., *Self and Identity* (New York: Wiley, 1987), 128.

16. Turner, "Articulating Self and Social Structure," 132.

17. N. K. Denzin, "Symbolic Interactionism and Ethnomethodology," in J. D. Douglas, ed., *Understanding Everyday Life: Toward the Reconstruction of Sociological Knowledge* (Chicago: Aldine Publishing Co., 1970).

18. See, for example, Baumeister, "Self and Identity: An Introduction."

19. D. Elkind, *The Hurried Child* (Boston: Addison-Wesley, 1981).

20. Harter, "Self and Identity Development."

21. D. P. McAdams, "The Case for Unity in the (Post)modern Self: A Modest Proposal," in R. D. Ashmore and L. Jussim, eds., *Self and Identity: Fundamental Issues* (New York: Oxford University Press, 1997).

22. Harter, "Self and Identity Development."

23. See, for example, S. K. Whitbourne, *The Me I Know: A Study of Adult Identity* (New York: Springer-Verlag, 1986).

24. M. B. Brewer, "The Social Self: On Being the Same and Different at the Same Time," *Personality and Social Psychology Bulletin* 17 (1991): 475–482.

25. B. Brown, "Peer Groups and Peer Cultures," in Feldman and Elliott, *At the Threshold.*

26. R. Josselson, "Identity and Relatedness in the Life Cycle," in H. A. Bosma, T. L. Graafsma, H. D. Grotevant, and D. J. de Levita, eds., *Identity and Development* (Thousand Oaks, CA: Sage, 1994).

27. S. Duck, L. West, and L. K. Acitelli, "Sewing the Field: The Tapestry of Relationships in Life and Research," in S. Duck, ed., *Handbook of Personal Relationships* (New York: Wiley, 1997).

28. Waterman, "Finding Something to Do or Someone to Be," 148.

29. Ibid., 149.

30. J. Marcia, "Identity in Adolescence," in J. Adelson, ed., *Handbook of Adolescent Psychology* (New York: Wiley, 1980).

31. Waterman, "Two Conceptions of Happiness."

32. Ibid.

33. R. C. Mannell and D. A. Kleiber, *A Social Psychology of Leisure* (State College, PA: Venture Press, 1997).

34. J. R. Kelly, *Leisure Identities and Interactions* (London: Allen & Unwin, 1983).

35. J. Reeve, "The Face of Interest," *Motivation and Emotion* 17 (1993): 353–375.

36. G. Bateson, *Steps to an Ecology of Mind* (New York: Ballantine Books, 1972).

37. R. May, *Freedom and Destiny* (New York City: W. W. Norton, 1981).

38. Larson, "Secrets in the Bedroom."

39. L. M. Haggard and D. R. Williams, "Self-Identity Benefits of Leisure Activities," in B. L. Driver, P. J. Brown, and G. L. Peterson, eds., *Benefits of Leisure* (State College, PA: Venture Publishing, 1991), 112; L. M. Haggard

and D. R. Williams, "Identity Affirmation Through Leisure Activities: Leisure Symbols of the Self," *Journal of Leisure Research* 24 (1992): 1–18.

40. Haggard and Williams, "Identity Affirmation."

41. F. Dimanche and D. Samdahl, "Leisure as Symbolic Consumption: A Conceptualization and Prospectus for Future Research," *Leisure Sciences* 16 (1994): 119–129.

42. C. Rojek, "De-differentiation and Leisure," *Society and Leisure* 16 (1993): 15–29; T. Veblen, *The Theory of the Leisure Class* (New York: New American Library, 1963).

43. S. Iso-Ahola, D. LaVerde, and A. R. Graefe, "Perceived Competence as a Mediator of the Relationship Between High Risk Sports Participation and Self-Esteem," *Journal of Leisure Research* 21 (1989): 32–39.

44. M. Csikszentmihalyi, *Flow: The Psychology of Optimal Experience* (New York: Harper Perennial, 1990); *The Evolving Self: A Psychology for the Third Millennium* (New York: HarperCollins, 1993).

45. A. W. Chickering, *Education and Identity* (San Francisco: Jossey-Bass, 1969); S. Danish, A. D'Augelli, and M. Ginsburg, "Life-Development Intervention: Promotion of Mental Health Through the Development of Competence," in S. Brown and R. Lent, eds., *Handbook of Counseling Psychology* (New York: Wiley, 1984).

46. Csikszentmihalyi, *The Evolving Self.*

47. Erikson, *Identity: Youth and Crisis*; Erikson, *Identity and the Life Cycle*; E. Erikson, *Childhood and Society* (New York: Norton, 1963).

48. Erikson, *Identity and the Life Cycle*, 116.

49. As noted earlier, the fact that leisure activities are often offered in response to open-ended identity questions (e.g., "How would you describe yourself?") led Gerald Adams and his colleagues to modify an inventory commonly used to assess identity status (G. R. Adams, J. Shea, and S. A. Fitch, "Toward the Development of an Objective Assessment of Ego-identity Status," *Journal of Youth and Adolescence* 9 [1979]: 223–237) to include the domain of recreation along with vocation, ideology, religion, and others (personal communication, March 1995).

50. R. Stebbins, *Amateurs, Professionals, and Serious Leisure* (Montreal: McGill-Queen's University Press, 1992).

51. Shamir, "Some Correlates of Leisure Identity Salience."

52. J. Grieves, "Acquiring a Leisure Identity: Juvenile Jazz Bands and the Moral Universe of 'Healthy' Leisure Time," *Leisure Studies* 8 (1989): 1–9.

53. G. A. Fine, *With the Boys: Little League Baseball and Preadolescent Culture* (Chicago: University of Chicago Press, 1987).

54. H. Grotevant, "The Integrative Nature of Identity: Bringing the Soloists to Sing in the Choir," in J. Kroger, ed., *Discussions on Ego Identity* (Hillsdale, NJ: Lawrence Erlbaum Publishers, 1993).

55. J. Hattie, H. W. Marsh, J. T. Neill, and G. E. Richards, "Adventure Education and Outward Bound: Out-of-Class Experiences That Make a Lasting Difference," *Review of Educational Research* 67 (1997): 43–87.

56. A. McCabe, B. Roberts, and T. Morris, "Athletic Activity, Body Image and Adolescent Identity," in L. Diamant, ed., *Mind-Body Maturity: Psychological Approaches to Sports, Exercise, and Fitness* (New York: Hemisphere, 1991).

57. D. Groff, "The Relationship Between Identity Formation and Participation in a Disabled Sports Program" (Doctoral dissertation, University of Georgia, Athens, GA, 1998); T. Williams, "Disability Sport Socialization and Identity Construction," *Adapted Physical Activity Quarterly* 11 (1994): 14–31.

58. R. Silbereisen, K. Eyferth, and G. Rudinger, *Development as Action in Context: Problem Behavior and Normal Youth Development* (New York: Springer-Verlag, 1986).

59. M. Csikszentmihalyi and R. Larson, *Being Adolescent* (New York: Basic Books, 1984).

60. Erikson, *Identity and the Life Cycle.*

61. M. Csikszentmihalyi and R. Larson, "Intrinsic Rewards in School Crime," *Crime and Delinquency* 24 (1978): 322–335.

62. I. Sato, "*Bosozoku*: Flow in Japanese Motorcycle Gangs," in M. Csikszentmihalyi and I. Csikszentmihalyi, eds., *Optimal Experience: Psychological Studies of Flow in Consciousness* (New York: Cambridge University Press, 1988).

63. D. Kleiber and C. Kirshnit, "Sport Involvement and Identity Formation," in L. Diamant, ed., *Mind-Body Maturity* (New York: Hemisphere, 1991).

64. For more on this point, see D. Kleiber, "Motivational Reorientation in Adulthood and the Resource of Leisure," in D. Kleiber and M. Maehr, eds., *Motivation and Adulthood* (Greenwich, CT: JAI Press, 1985).

65. B. D. Kivel, "In on the Outside, Out on the Inside: Lesbian/Gay/Bisexual Youth, Identity, and Leisure" (Doctoral dissertation, University of Georgia, Athens, GA, 1996).

66. Baumeister, *Identity*, 137–138.

67. K. Gergen, *The Saturated Self: Dilemmas of Identity in Contemporary Life* (New York: Basic Books, 1991).

68. J. Dowd, "An Act Made Perfect in Habit: The Self in the Postmodern Age," *Current Perspectives in Social Theory* 16 (1996): 237–263.

69. McAdams, "The Case for Unity in the (Post)modern Self."

70. B. Kingsolver, *High Tide in Tucson* (New York: HarperCollins, 1996), 131.

6 Personal Expressiveness and the Transcendence of Negative Life Events

No one can go back and make a brand new start, my friend. But anyone can start from here and make a brand new end.

—Dave, a head injury survivor[1]

I believe that the study of history is largely lost on high school students; it seems much more intrinsically interesting in college or in the course of adult education, when one has a history of one's own. This has been my experience, anyway. Certainly there have been better high school history students than I was. But the power of retrospection—and the concomitant appreciation of history—seems to emerge naturally only when childhood begins to recede in the rearview mirror.

The resolution of the problem of identity formation that we addressed in the previous chapter comes in part with a recognition of one's personal story. We enter adulthood with a multiplicity of identity attributes that together constitute who we believe we are. These attributes are formed and expressed in various life contexts, including leisure. Reconciling these sometimes conflicting identity images and making sense of personal experiences (including those that are painful) contributes to the creation of a coherent sense of self.[2] While differentiation is important in the course of identity formation, it is integration of the various identity elements over time that brings about some coherence. Coherence is a matter of degree, of course, and it varies considerably from one person to the next. And even in the best case, coherence is temporary, as life-course changes create the continuing need for revision in the identity that has been constructed. Nevertheless, coherence of self is an important source of stability as one negotiates the predictable developmental tasks and role changes of adulthood.

The concept of *life story*, or personal narrative, has much in common with the idea of identity. But a personal narrative offers more of a time frame; it reflects the past, present, and future as well as one's temperament, values, purposes, place in the life course, and experience of sociohistorical events.[3] The self-definition of a young adult emerges in narrative form from the perspective of personal history and a sense of future opportunities. A life story is an identity with an elaborated past and an articulated future. While this process of narrative construction may not begin until adulthood, the early chapters of one's life story are clearly situated in childhood.

Both identity and the life story represent the workings of hierarchical integration in making meaning of the various threads of experience that the process of differentiation has created. But development continues in ways that will challenge the coherence of the existing structure of a young person's sense of self, even when changes can be anticipated. The course of socialization reviewed in Chapters 3 and 4 does not end with adolescence but responds to the changing role requirements of adulthood. Young people may anticipate graduation, but they cannot fully understand or be prepared for the realities of being out of school, marrying, starting a career, and raising a child. Each such event will create the need for reorganization of the life story that is being composed.[4]

Negative Life Events

Among life's unanticipated events, some come as a great shock—a life-threatening illness, the loss of a child, a devastating fire. Even positive events, such as an unexpected promotion or a distant aunt's surprise bequest, can be disruptive to one's sense of self, though not usually to the extent of negative life events.[5] And both negative and positive events can precipitate development. The differentiation that occurs initially in such cases is the result of externally created disorganization rather than individual choice, but people often take serious disruptions and even tragedies as signals to make radical changes.[6] A friend's recent and unexpected heart attack was a sobering reminder to him—and others—to appreciate life for what it offers and to recognize what is most important. He reduced his workload and exercised more, but it was being with his family that became most important to him. Responses like this have been associated with a wide variety of illnesses, including cancer.[7] The image of a "phoenix rising from the ashes" is often evoked in such cases;[8] but even with less traumatic cases, the disintegration caused by such events creates the conditions for differentiation and new levels of integration and makes individuals more open to personality change.[9] The word *transformation* applies to such changes.

In *Flow: The Psychology of Optimal Experience,* Mihaly Csikszentmihalyi referred to several examples of such personal transformations as "cheating chaos."[10] He pointed to work in Milan, Italy, with individuals who had lost the use of limbs and had identified their accidents as being both the most negative and the most positive events in their lives. It is not uncommon to hear a victim of a negative life event refer to it as "the best thing that ever happened to me." Csikszentmihalyi related this reaction in part to the event's *focusing* effect. The limitations of the handicap focus effort and skill. Facing the demands of coping, a person is able to clarify goals and reduce contradictory alternatives; and the functional effectiveness that is cultivated can be flow-producing and rewarding. Learning to live again in a new way, focusing on what the environment affords, and developing the skills necessary to survive and grow becomes a source of enjoyment and pride in many cases.

Initially, such events have the effect of stopping the individuals in their tracks and causing them to reevaluate their lives. Even before effective recovery actions are taken, victims of negative life events respond to the stress, the loss of competence, and the forced self-appraisal by examining the ways in which their lives will and should change or remain the same.[11]

The problem to be addressed in this chapter, then, is the challenge of transcending those life events that are serious disruptions to an emerging life story. Leisure comes into play both in the experience of loss and, often, in the course of adjustment and transformation. Play, recreation, and leisure activity have long been used in the treatment of trauma and illness, and we will consider some of evidence of their effective use in the course of adjustment and rehabilitation; but the focus here, as with the rest of the book, is on development.

In Chapter 5 I suggested that leisure provides a context for identity formation by allowing for contemplation of possibilities, experimentation with those possibilities, and commitment to meaningful patterns of personal expression. Activities that reflect individual potentials, that produce the intense involvement of flow-type experience, and that involve commitment to others who take the activity seriously were described as *personally expressive*[12] and as being most influential in identity formation. The thesis of this chapter is that such activities and experiences are at least as important for transcending the impacts of negative life events.

It is well known that artists often find their inspiration through suffering.[13] Their art allows them to bring some order and meaning to affliction. But others, too, respond to the stress and disorder of negative life events by creating patterns of personal expressiveness. Becoming functionally effective, first in necessary ways and then in personally expressive ways, is often experienced as a triumph over adversity, an epiphany, in directing the unfolding of a revised life story.

Among the many possible negative life events that can befall a person, we will focus on two that are more common in early adulthood: spinal-cord injury and date rape. They can both be enormously disruptive to the personal patterns, relationships, and even identities of those involved. Leisure experience is significant in the nature of the disruption itself, in the process of adjustment, and in the course of personal transformation.

My interest in spinal-cord injury emerged out of studies of the impact of career-ending injuries on elite athletes and the need to assess whether certain effects could be generalized to a "noncelebrated" population that experienced even more serious injuries. While it might be expected that the celebrated athlete would experience some turmoil in leaving the exciting life of sport, our findings fit with those of others who established that the transition was not as difficult as some would have predicted.[14] Being able to anticipate the end seems to allow most athletes to prepare for and make the transition relatively easily, the few exceptions being those who are especially focused and/or particularly idolized. But an unexpected and premature exit from sport—as with a career-ending injury—is disorienting and distressing to anyone who has been seriously committed to that activity. The loss of highly developed patterns of personal expressiveness results in illness that is as much existential as physical.[15] Colleagues who are specialists in therapeutic recreation subsequently convinced me that individuals who had been disabled by spinal-cord injury would provide additional insight into the significance of personal expressiveness in both illness and rehabilitation.

The subject of date rape was addressed by another colleague, Robin Yaffe, who was able to gain the confidence of date-rape victims who consented to tell her their stories.[16] Like spinal-cord injury, date rape includes a physical assault, but the similarities seem to end there. Since date rape is not usually "visible" after the fact, it rarely draws continued public attention or even the same degree of attention from the therapeutic community. Indeed, victims usually seek a distancing anonymity from the event. Nevertheless, both events breed a sense of loss that runs deeper than the immediate recovery process suggests. A rupturing of identity is characteristic of both. Each calls for a restructuring of one's beliefs, values, sense of self, and life goals in ways that make sense of the experience.

The next section addresses more closely the relevance of leisure in the illness experience and the role that it plays in helping individuals adjust to their traumas and recast their life stories to create optimism and a sense of coherence. After this general discussion, we will consider case-study data on both spinal-cord injury and date rape.

The Relevance of Leisure in Negative Life Events

As noted earlier, the context of leisure is an opportunity for a wide range of experiences, from trivial self-indulgence to escape to self-expanding personal expressiveness. The ways of incorporating activity into treatment for rehabilitation purposes are nearly as varied. But research on rehabilitation often neglects the ways in which leisure is involved in the illness itself. Nor has sufficient consideration been given to leisure's place in long-term adjustment and personal change.

Most studies of negative life events focus on their impact in undermining instrumental resources, particularly physical health and economic security. But if leisure experience and personal expressiveness are important in the course of socialization and identity formation, it follows that the compromising of these sources of meaning and well-being will be a significant part of the experience of loss. Indeed, the experience of "illness" that accompanies such events often centers on the disruption of patterns of enjoyment and self-expression and of the relationships in which they are embedded.

Also neglected in rehabilitation practice and research is the relevance of leisure in life story reconstruction following negative life events. This lack of attention is due in part to an emphasis on restoring that which has been lost rather than on coming to terms with the reality of the loss and considering possibilities for reorganization and redirection. Restoring continuity is usually a priority for the individual affected and for those friends, family, and professionals in a position to help, with little attention being given to whether the activity fits with an altered conception of self. Understanding that "all is not lost" requires considering what aspects of oneself remain in spite of the event. Nevertheless, there is evidence that a reconstruction of the self can result from a significant disruption of one's life. Personal expressiveness often leads the way in that regard. Constructing a future that is both enjoyable and meaningful becomes a mission in some cases.

Leisure experience is most often used to try to get back to "normal." This is the usual orientation of both those enduring the traumatic event and those with the responsibility of helping them through it. Activities are adopted for their power to distract from either the feeling of physical pain or associated psychological distress. This strategy is generally referred to as *emotion-focused coping*.[17] A related idea is to use leisure as a social space to reconnect with others in familiar activities that restore a sense of continuity even if involvement in such activities has to be modified in important ways. This response can steady a person undergoing a destabilizing experience. In a study of people with spinal-cord injury, Karen Yoshida illustrates the point with the example of a young man who had recently been paralyzed, and, after an extremely distressing rehabilitation period, was taken from the hospital by family members to their cabin in the woods. His growing enthusiasm along the way there signaled to him that life was still worth living, something he had questioned often since his injury.[18]

As noted in Chapter 5 and earlier, leisure experience contributes the most to an identity when activities are intensely involving and result in increased competence. Activities taken seriously enough to produce flow-type experience are valued as personally expressive and meaningful in ways that more casual activities are not. Commitment to an activity and to people associated with it results in the integration of that activity and related interests into a sense of self. Accordingly, failure to continue such activities can be at least as threatening to one's identity as the loss of more instrumental functions. In Yoshida's study of spinal-cord injury, the inability to return to dancing was traumatic for a professional dancer, but it forced him to come to terms with his disability and the possibilities that remained. By recognizing that he could live well despite physical limitations, he was able to shift his attention to finding sources of self-expression that he could embrace as passionately, if not as physically, as his former occupation.

In spite of such examples, the literature on coping with negative life events is largely devoid of attention to leisure experiences. This is even more remarkable in view of the extensive use of leisure activities by occupational and recreational therapists and other clinicians, and the abundant evidence that activity can be helpful in coping.[19] Perhaps this is the all-too-familiar prejudice that views play, recreation, and leisure activity as trivial aspects of life, or maybe it simply reflects the recognition that repairing disrupted role relationships (i.e., those related to work and family) is far more important to mental and physical health.[20] If leisure activities are important in one's life story, however, it is necessary to attend both to their significance in the distress incurred and to their potential value in the course of rehabilitation.

A related question, and one of practical significance as well, is the value of reestablishing a personal narrative as seamlessly as possible after a negative life event versus using the event as a symbolic vehicle for transcending one's previous existence in ways previously unimagined. In the former case, continuity is the priority and "reconnecting" is the metaphor of action; the latter reflects the value and priority of discontinuity and *restorying*.[21] In either case, leisure is relevant to adjustment and rehabilitation, especially those activities that are personally expressive, generating meaning and direction. Such activities are also likely to nurture feelings of competence, control, and freedom that can moderate the impact of stress on illness.[22] But leisure can also serve as a *buffer* such that even trivial and escapist activity may allow one to manage the pain and distress to some extent, and/or a network of others may offer social support and distraction.[23]

Escapist activity, like the time-wasting or self-indulgent activities discussed in the last two chapters, is not highly valued by researchers or the general public. However, the need for escape in highly stressful situations has been borne out in a wide variety of clinical studies. Some form of emotion-focused (rather than "problem-focused") coping, avoiding dealing directly with the source of pain, is generally regarded as adaptive for an initial period.[24] Escapist activities may reflect a degree of denial that can be maladaptive and psychopathological over extended periods; but denial may be necessary in holding one's internal reality together for a while, thus allowing the person to cope with and focus on the more basic demands of daily living. Put more simply, denial, distraction, and escape buy time in the early phases of adjustment to traumatic life events.

Negative Life Events:
Loss of Leisure, Loss of Self

As mentioned earlier, I became more interested in the relevance of leisure to negative life events after finding that elite athletes seemed to be least successful in adjusting to their retirement from sport when their careers were ended prematurely by injury.[25] We wondered if the effects were exclusive to sports or if the loss of personal expressiveness might be found in those who had suffered negative life events of other kinds.[26] We suspected that the disruption of the ability to engage in preferred activities, when those activities have special relevance to a person's identity, would be as distressful as the injury itself. While the general dynamics may apply to the loss of a job or the loss of a spouse, among other events, we focused our attention on people who had incurred a spinal-cord injury (SCI) that left them with some paralysis.

For an analytical framework, we used the work of Howard Brody,[27] who defined "illness" as a disruption to one's life narrative, where the future self imagined in the narrative is made doubtful by some perceived threat to one's health. Most illness experiences are acute, resulting in an experience of disruption in which the narrative is *suspended.* In such cases the threat to health is determined to be transient, permitting a return to the former narration of the life story. In the case of chronic illness or permanent disability, the disruption to the life story is one in which, to one degree or another, the imagined future self is fundamentally *altered.*

Yoshida's work with adults with SCI provided preliminary support for this position. Her findings suggested that SCI victims reconstruct their life stories in a "pendular" fashion, moving between their non-disabled and disabled aspects to integrate them in a coherent understanding of themselves in the past, present, and future. Most of Yoshida's subjects also referred to some valued leisure activity, context (e.g., involving family or friends), or identity that was at risk in the course of narrative reconstruction. Though some of these associations were profoundly negative (e.g., realizing he would never be able to dance again), while others were positive (e.g., realizing that by going to the cabin on the lake, "living was still possible"), they all represented striking turning points in her subjects' self-reconstruction—perhaps more so because other contexts for self-expression (e.g., work) were unavailable to them.[28]

In our own study of spinal-cord injury, interviews were conducted with informants both before and from three to five months after they were discharged. The data from the interview transcripts that related to the experience of the injury clustered mostly into two general themes: loss of ability and disruption of relationships. The second of these was also quite similar to a theme that Yaffe found in her study of victims of date rape, as we will see shortly.

Illness: Loss of Favored Abilities

Dealing with the loss of physical function was largely a matter of survival in the beginning, but as time passed, our informants were increasingly preoccupied with the loss of favored activities. For example, there was six-foot-five-inch Jonathan [pseudonym], who missed being able to "jump up there and slam that ball through that rim real hard" in recreational (church league) basketball. For Mike, it was his self-image as a do-it-yourselfer that was compromised:

> My log cabin's being built up there. I used to do all that stuff before, you know, driving nails. . . . I can't do that anymore. I have to let somebody else do that. I was going to do all the plumbing work myself, and I can't do that . . . so that's going to be an adjustment, you know.

Nor were lost abilities restricted to overtly physical activity. An unrequited enthusiasm for reading, being unable to "hold a book, read it, [and] turn pages," left Lynn struggling to learn how to use a mouthstick. Mastering the mouthstick became a challenge itself for her and ultimately a source of confidence, but her inability to read normally initially defined her injury experience.

Even as individuals proceeded through rehabilitation and gained a new sense of being able to continue with familiar activities, albeit in a modified form, there was still a sense of loss. Constraints often served to undermine the full level of satisfaction and enjoyment to be derived from an activity, as in this example:

It was great to go back fishing again, but at the same time . . . I can't cast as well, probably one out of five times I got the line in the water. And then one out of fifteen times was actually far enough out to fish. And besides, I couldn't bait my own hook, and I can't reel them in. But I mean for me fishing is everything; it's not just catching the fish, it's setting up to catch the fish and cleaning them and hooking them . . . that was the only thing that was kind of disappointing to me; I realized how much work I have to do now to be able to do all those things again.

These illustrations and the remaining data demonstrated to us that the loss of that easy, unself-conscious mind-body unity of leisure activities was one of the most significant aspects of the illness experience. What had become almost "second nature" was suddenly a collection of discrete, challenging acts, comparable to learning to dress oneself or use the restroom independently. These self-conscious efforts reflect dramatic changes in lifestyle that are experienced, at least initially, as a loss of freedom and leisure. Karla Henderson and her colleagues identified similar reactions in their studies of women who had become seriously ill or physically disabled.[29] Their respondents lamented the loss of spontaneity in their activities and the shrinkage of time that accompanied greater attention to the tasks of daily living, accentuated in some cases by problems with accessibility.

For some in our spinal-cord injury study, the loss of a leisure ability seemed to have as much to do with the social world within which it was embedded as with functional impairments per se. Before Rachel was injured, her passion for dancing included a particular way of dressing. Not only did she feel uncomfortable "dancing" in a motorized chair, she was also uncomfortable with the way she looked:

I just never dressed the way I'm dressing now. I wore jeans and cowboy boots, or I wore dresses and high heels; and this is different for me. I don't like wearing jogging pants and T-shirts and stuff. It's not the way I dress.

Her discomfort with how she now looked clearly undermined her experience of enjoyment. Body image and appearance are important aspects of identity for most people, and physical self-concept becomes especially threatened when one is limited to a wheelchair and physical self-expression is permanently altered.[30]

Illness: Disruption of Leisure Relationships

Rachel's experience also demonstrates the importance of the social context of the injury. In all the SCI cases examined, the experience of loss was a *social* matter as well. The power of the injury to change the lives and relationships of people was often illustrated with reference to leisure activities. While this applied to friends and family, spouses and significant others, and even pets, one of the more compelling illustrations came through the voice of a man who associated physical expressiveness with being a parent:

> My little boy, he loves baseball, and I feel that I can't really just give [that] to him like I want to. I'd rather swing the bat with my boy or catch a ball with him, and I just can't. I really miss that, and I feel like that's a part of my life that has just been taken away from me.

Friendships and peer groups were at risk as well. In one case, it was missing out on going to the mountains with a group of friends, while for Lynn, it was not being able to contribute in a group situation:

> I can't participate in a lot of things. I mean like this weekend, you know, they fed everybody the whole weekend, and I couldn't help with that. I mean I couldn't even feed myself. I can't wash dishes, I can't help or fix anything to take, you know. I don't feel like I'm contributing at all.

Being "a part of things" is much of what people appreciate about leisure activities. Clearly, the disruption of relationships parallels, accentuates, and may even supersede in importance the loss of well-learned physical skills in enjoyable activities. And where enjoyable activities are largely shared prior to injury, changes in both activities and relationships result in a *compounded* sense of loss.

Yaffe's study of date rape victims led her to similar findings with respect to what was lost in the experience of being raped by an acquaintance. *Disrupted sociability* was one of three principal categories that emerged from her interviews with women who had this experience. The ability to be relaxed and comfortable around men in dating situations was seriously impaired for these women. For example, Jill indicated that when she was on a date subsequent to being raped she was "extremely vigilant and uptight, reacting to the least touch (hand on a shoulder or back) by withdrawing both physically and emotionally, whether there had been any sexual intent by the male at that point or not." And for Adrienne, the effect was more general:

> I rarely date any more since I have not had a successful relationship since. . . . I question everybody's intentions. Always. I have thrown myself 150% into my work, and I don't have that much of a social life. I am frightened of meeting new people—I don't tend to make friends, they tend to make friends with me. And then I wonder what they want.

As with the spinal-cord injury cases, the women in the date-rape study demonstrated that the loss of relaxed sociability is significant in defining the illness they experienced. As a result of their ordeals, both groups found leisure to be compromised and undermined, a feeling of loss that pervaded other aspects of their lives as well.

Leisure Restored and Lives Restoried

If the leisure of victims of negative life events can be characterized as having some personal expressiveness before the traumatic events occurred, such experience is often only a faint hope in the early phases of adjustment. In the studies of people with spinal-cord injury and women who had experienced date rape, personally expressive aspects of leisure were largely irrelevant in the early stages of adjustment, except in identifying what had been lost. And free time itself can be more of an enemy than a friend, as Yaffe found with the women she interviewed. Nevertheless, though it begs the question of the freedom generally associated with leisure, any activity that could be distracting was appreciated.

Vehicles of escape was the name Yaffe gave to this category of experience that emerged from her data. Activities that could take the mind off the traumatic event, however destructive the activities may have been in other respects, were a first-order solution for all of the women involved. A variety of strategies were used, as these two examples illustrate:

I would use daydreaming, exercise and dieting to "keep at bay" painful feelings or memories. I remember doing some ritual of exercise—swimming, trampolining, jogging, and/or aerobics for 60 minutes a day, without fail. I was very disciplined. . . . I was very sad.

What I really enjoyed was escaping from my everyday existence, which I hated, so anything that offered me an alternative reality was OK. I smoked a little pot, but never did any other drugs. I just didn't like who I was and how my life was going, so I spent a lot of time trying to forget about it.

There was less of this kind of escapist behavior reflected in the interviews with those with spinal-cord injuries, probably because they found themselves rather immediately in the context of rehabilitation services that were highly supervised. The date-rape victims, in contrast, were left largely to their own devices (or "vehicles," to use Yaffe's word). The course of treatment for those with spinal-cord injuries was defined primarily to help them locate a pathway to reestablishing themselves, reminding them at the outset that all is not lost and that they have options that may well include the interests they had prior to the injury. As was previously mentioned, the course of rehabilitation is typically directed toward the resumption of activity in spite of some of the most apparently debilitating injuries. Even with paralysis in both legs, wheelchair basketball is possible, for example, and adaptive technology has been developed to the point that most activities can be renewed in some form for those with at least some use of their limbs. The resumption of familiar activities was both the hope of most SCI patients and a common objective of the therapists who treated them, as our transcripts revealed.[31] One of our respondents, Mark, allowed for the fact that the activities associated with hunting would likely take longer than before, but he was looking forward to doing it all again anyway. Similarly, James, who had been injured in a truck accident and faced the prospect of abandoning his enthusiasm for shop work, realized that that wasn't necessary:

I'm not going to let it [the injury] dictate the way I live. I might make some changes, and I might be on a lower level or less visible level, but basically I'm going to do what I did all along. I can still sit up at the shop and cut and polish stones.

But is continuity the best alternative? Might it not be better to treat the disrupted narrative as an opportunity to change, to become something different? If we regard people as intentional beings, capable of authoring a life story, however influenced it may be by circumstances, then a disruption allows for a "rewrite" of the story.[32] And given the *relative* freedom of the context of leisure, if such "restorying" is to happen, leisure may afford the best starting point. The most powerful impact, of course, would likely come from those activities that are personally expressive, that involve some degree of commitment, seriousness, and identification with others.

The Italian study of the effects of spinal-cord injury discussed by Csikszentmihalyi suggests that life after a traumatic and disabling injury might be transformed in leisure activity.[33] He referred to a motorcycle accident victim, Lucio, who found flow, enjoyment, and ultimately public acclaim in becoming a world-class archer after his injury. And then there was Franco, who was able to substitute a pre-injury passion for acrobatic dancing with interests in wheelchair sports, the guitar, and chess. In chess, he went on to become a national champion. Such success stories may be exceptional, but it is the personal transformation that is most noteworthy here.

For others, though, the embracing of leisure may be more global. In a study of brain injury survivors,[34] a former "workaholic" who had been unable to work since her head injury expressed the struggle she faced in overcoming society's prescription that work is necessary to be a "good person" in our culture today:

> That word "work" is a problem . . . one part of me says that if I could only be normal again ([laughs], yeah, my brain, my intellect knows better, but the gut once in a while revolts). . . . Well, if I could just work I'd be normal. The other side is there are more and more days where I say, "God, its nice to think I don't have to work anymore. How lucky I am."

This woman's life story was clearly at a turning point, and the prospect of being something different seemed to coincide with a new awareness of leisure.

Our own studies of individuals with spinal-cord injury did not provide much evidence of the need or tendency for transformative restorying; but since our second interviews occurred soon after the patients' release from treatment, we didn't fully capture the totality of the transition period. Still, our study reflected some possible limitations to the continuity theme in another category of illness experience we called "relapse." After the patients left the rehabilitation setting, the absence of a treatment milieu and a patient cohort frequently brought into question the viability of resuming old familiar activities. Indeed, in some cases the illness experience seemed to reassert itself in a manner reflected in Donald's observations:

> When I was down at [the center], I was real active due to the fact that there were other people around with handicaps who understood how I felt. And then when you come home and you have to do it by yourself, it's hard. And that's what triggered me to just shut everybody out, shut myself out. I didn't get up every morning and go out and see fifty wheelchairs running around. There was just one.

In some contrast, Yaffe's study of date-rape victims, which took place retrospectively (between five and ten years after the rape occurrences), afforded her respondents a longer time in which to make adjustments and gain perspective, and the interview data led her to identify a third category, which she referred to as *vehicles of reintegration*. This category included meeting and getting to know new people, initiating new volunteer activities, and entering into new social arrangements, all different from what was done before the rape experience. Jean and Marianne provide variations on the theme:

> In Michigan, I did everything I hadn't done in Europe—i.e., I forced myself to make friends and not be so actively self-conscious. I had a party soon after I moved to Michigan, one of my first, and since have become a very active hostess. I hadn't thought about this before, but I think this has been one way of dealing with the sense of helplessness I had felt during and after the rape. This has allowed me to positively control my social surroundings. I like social crowds much more now than before and find that I can be charming and fun in groups in ways which I had never imagined before.

> I became very close friends with a woman in my graduate program. We worked out together, shopped, gossiped, etc. This friendship in many ways saved me. That summer we drove around Delaware a lot and just had fun. I've described it since as "being 14 again but with money and a

car." I began to pay much more attention to fashion, etc. than I ever had before. I've always been a fairly serious student; that summer I let myself be a girlie girl, and I enjoyed it quite a bit.

Jean's comments may reveal more personal expressiveness, as we have defined it, than the traveling Marianne, but there is evidence in both cases (and others among Yaffe's respondents) of a degree of personal transcendence reflected in newly recognized interests and talents. Had we followed up with the spinal-cord injury group, perhaps we would have found more of what Csikszentmihalyi identified in the cases of Lucio and Franco, discussed earlier. If so, they would add more evidence in support of the contention that negative life events often lead to some personal reevaluation and to a sharpened appreciation of the opportunities we have to make the most of the life we have left.

Conclusion

The *experience* of negative life events is commonly associated with the disruption of patterns of personal expressiveness and sociability. Beyond that, the course of resuming or reconstructing a coherent narrative may involve periods of escapist activity—especially in the absence of social support—that are emotionally necessary, if not particularly meaningful. Ultimately, in many cases, personal expressiveness becomes important in the adjustment process. Whether such expressiveness involves reconnecting with the self that was temporarily "lost" or in setting a new direction for a new self, or perhaps some combination of those, it may be the most important process in enabling one to carry on with hope and appreciation for life itself.

Notes

1. S. L. Hutchinson, "An Exploration of the Processes of Self-Identity Reconstruction by People Who Acquired a Brain Injury" (Master's thesis, Dalhousie University, Halifax, Nova Scotia, 1996).

2. While this idea is well established in identity research, it is reconciled with postmodernism to some extent in D. P. McAdams, "The Case for Unity in the (Post)Modern Self," in R. D. Ashmore and L. Jussim, eds., *Self and Identity: Fundamental Issues* (New York: Oxford University Press, 1997).

3. B. J. Cohler, "Personal Narrative and the Life Course," *Life-Span Development and Behavior*, vol. 4. (New York: Academic Press, 1982); and

"Life-Course Perspectives on the Study of Adversity, Stress, and Coping: Discussion of Papers from the West Virginia Conference," in E. M. Cummings, A. L. Greene, and K. H. Karraker, eds., *Life-Span Developmental Psychology: Perspectives on Stress and Coping* (Hillsdale, NJ: Lawrence Erlbaum, 1991).

4. The idea of a life story is, of course, a metaphor, adding a time dimension to one's identity, and people vary in both their awareness of self in time and in their tendency to articulate that awareness for themselves and others. An example of how the idea is captured in narrative analysis research and used by individuals themselves can be found in Mary Catherine Bateson's *Composing a Life* (New York: Penguin Books, 1990).

5. R. C. Kessler, R. H. Price, and C. B. Wortman, "Social Factors in Psychopathology: Stress, Social Support and Coping Processes," *Annual Review of Psychology* 36 (1985): 531–572; P. Thoits, "Dimensions of Life Events that Influence Psychological Distress: An Evaluation and Synthesis of the Literature," in H. Kaplan, ed., *Psychosocial Stress: Trends in Theory and Research* (New York: Wiley, 1983).

6. R. Janoff-Bulman and C. Timko, "Coping with Traumatic Life Events: The Role of Denial in Light of People's Assumptive Worlds," in C. R. Snyder and C. E. Ford, eds., *Coping with Negative Life Events* (New York: Plenum, 1987).

7. Ibid.

8. A. J. Stewart and J. M. Healy, "Personality and Adaptation to Change," in R. Hogan and W. Jones, eds., *Perspectives in Personality,* vol.1 (New York: JAI Press, 1985).

9. K. J. Kiecolt, "Stress and the Decision to Change Oneself: A Theoretical Model," *Social Psychology Quarterly* 57 (1994): 49–63.

10. M. Csikszentmihalyi, *Flow: The Psychology of Optimal Experience* (New York: Harper Perennial, 1990).

11. Kiecolt, "Stress and the Decision to Change Oneself."

12. A. S. Waterman, "Personal Expressiveness: Philosophical and Psychological Foundations," *Journal of Mind and Behavior* 11 (1990): 47–74; "Two Conceptions of Happiness: Contrasts of Personal Expressiveness (Eudaimonia) and Hedonic Enjoyment," *Journal of Personality and Social Psychology* 64 (1993): 678–693.

13. M. Csikszentmihalyi, *The Evolving Self: A Psychology for the Third Millennium* (New York: HarperCollins, 1993); personal communication.

14. J. J. Coakley, "Leaving Competitive Sport: Retirement or Rebirth?" *Quest* 35 (1983): 1–11.

15. S. C. Brock and D. A. Kleiber, "Narratives in Medicine: The Stories of Elite College Athletes' Career-Ending Injuries," *Qualitative Health Research* 4 (1994): 411–430.

16. R. Yaffe, "Leisure and Adjustment to Date Rape" (Doctoral dissertation, University of Georgia, Athens, GA, 1996).

17. Janoff-Bulman and C. Timko, "Coping with Traumatic Life Events"; R. S. Lazarus and S. Folkman, *Stress, Appraisal, and Coping* (New York: Springer Publishing, 1984).

18. K. K. Yoshida, "Reshaping of Self: A Pendular Reconstruction of Self and Identity Among Adults with Traumatic Spinal Cord Injuries," *Sociology of Health and Illness* 15 (1993): 217–245.

19. D. Coleman, "Leisure Based Social Support, Leisure Dispositions and Health," *Journal of Leisure Research* 25 (1993): 350–361; J. W. Reich and A. Zautra, "Life Events and Personal Causation: Some Relationships with Satisfaction and Distress," *Journal of Health and Social Behavior* 41 (1981): 1002–1012; R. J. Wheeler and M. A. Frank, "Identification of Stress Buffers," *Behavioral Medicine* 14 (1988): 78–89.

20. An exception is Prigatano's (1989) work on play patterns as sources of individuation and self-expression in brain-injured patients: G. P. Prigatano, "Work, Love, and Play After Brain Injury," *Bulletin of the Menninger Clinic* 53 (1989): 414–431.

21. Brock and Kleiber, "Narratives in Medicine"; D. Kleiber, S. Brock, J. Dattilo, Y. Lee, and L. Caldwell, "The Relevance of Leisure in an Illness Experience: Realities of Spinal Cord Injury," *Journal of Leisure Research* 27 (1995): 283–299.

22. D. Coleman and S. Iso-Ahola, "Leisure and Health: The Role of Social Support and Self-determination," *Journal of Leisure Research* 25 (1993): 111–128.

23. D. Kleiber, "Motivational Reorientation in Adulthood and the Resource of Leisure," in D. Kleiber and M. Maehr, eds., *Motivation and Adulthood* (Greenwich, CT: JAI Press, 1985); see also Coleman and Iso-Ahola, "Leisure and Health."

24. Janoff-Bulman and Timko, "Coping with Traumatic Life Events."

25. Brock and Kleiber, "Narratives in Medicine"; D. A. Kleiber and S. C. Brock, "The Effect of Career-Ending Injuries on the Subsequent Well-Being of Elite College Athletes," *Sociology of Sport Journal* 9 (1992): 70–75.

26. Kleiber et al., "The Relevance of Leisure in an Illness Experience."

27. H. Brody, *Stories of Sickness* (New Haven, CT: Yale University Press, 1987).

28. Yoshida, "Reshaping of Self."

29. K. A. Henderson, L. A. Bedini, L. Hecht, and R. Shuler, "Women with Physical Disabilities and the Negotiation of Leisure Constraints," *Leisure Studies* 14 (1995): 17–31.

30. K. A. Henderson, L. A. Bedini, and L. Hecht, "Not Just a Wheelchair, Not Just a Woman: Self-Identity and Leisure," *Therapeutic Recreation Journal* 2 (1994): 73–86.

31. Y. Lee, J. Dattilo, D. Kleiber, and L. Caldwell, "Exploring the Meaning of Continuity of Recreation Activity in the Early Stages of Adjustment for People with Spinal Cord Injuries," *Leisure Sciences* 18 (1996): 209–225.

32. Brock and Kleiber, "Narratives in Medicine."

33. Csikszentmihalyi, *Flow.*

34. Hutchinson, "An Exploration of the Processes of Self-Identity Reconstruction."

7 *Self-Renewal and Generativity in Middle Age*

Whether or not one experiences seriously disruptive events, such as those discussed in Chapter 6, change can be expected throughout the life span. For some people the changes are modest and superficial; aging for them is largely a matter of expanding the wardrobe of role-related apparel in dressing a stable personality. Adulthood in such cases represents a kind of plateau after the ascent through childhood and adolescence and before the onset of decline in later life. But this pattern is more the exception than the rule; adult development research indicates that change occurs throughout life, and not just in response to significant events and changes in circumstances.[1] Though life events such as the loss of a parent or a divorce often trigger personal change, sometimes something as simple as a dream, a conversation with a friend, or an engaging novel will precipitate movement for a person who is ready to make a change. A friend of my wife's referred to it as sitting in her "life chair": "Sometimes you feel relaxed and almost one with the chair as it supports you; other times you feel perched on the edge, ready to leap out of it at the slightest push." Midlife, more than any other period, is a time of such readiness.

Midlife brings a sense of unease for many people. The loss of youthful appearance and accompanying feelings of diminished physical attractiveness, career disillusionment, relationship problems, bod-

Portions of this chapter appeared in D. A. Kleiber and R. O. Ray, "Leisure and Generativity," in J. R. Kelly, ed., *Activity and Aging* (Newbury Park, CA: Sage, 1993). Reprinted with permission.

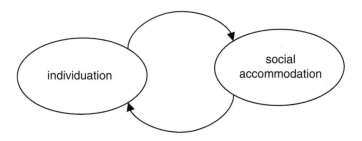

FIGURE 7.1
Individual-Society Dialectic

ily changes, changes in sexual activity, aging and dying parents, and changing relationships with children are among the conditions that commonly contribute to symptoms of restlessness, irritability, boredom, stagnation, angst about the future, and other more dramatic symptoms of a midlife crisis.[2] These symptoms are all associated with an expanding awareness of a limited future. One's age becomes defined by life left to live rather than years since birth.[3] But people react very differently to this awareness, from resigned acceptance, leading to an extended period of stagnation, to a rather sudden reorganization of priorities. Although personality characteristics may be relatively stable and unchanging, concerns and purposes that define a person's identity and shape the story yet to unfold can change dramatically.

In this chapter we address those issues of midlife that reflect an essential conflict between individual self-expression and social responsiveness. While these two purposes are not always incompatible, they do tend to be addressed dialectically; in other words, the overemphasis on one requires an adjustment in the other direction, as Figure 7.1 suggests. Erik Erikson and Daniel Levinson have given special attention to this subject, and yet they see the problem rather differently.

Levinson makes the case that the successful resolution of midlife issues comes primarily in freeing oneself from excessive social concern, whereas Erikson establishes social commitment as the developmentally appropriate turn in life once individual intimacy has been achieved. Both of these views deserve attention since leisure experience is relevant to each, and the picture of midlife development may be sketched more completely by considering them together. Let us begin with Levinson's perspective and those who share this point of view.

Individuation and Self-Renewal

Recently, the word "middlessence" has been introduced to characterize current middle-agers.[4] The obvious association with adolescence may be appropriate for a number of reasons. Essays on contemporary American society have been particularly critical of the narcissism of many adults, particularly baby boomers who are now in their forties and early fifties.[5] However, while regressive self-indulgence and self-absorption may describe some of the current cohort of middle-agers in North America, the similarity of middle age to adolescence has deeper and more positive roots.

The onset of middle age, like the onset of adolescence, often brings about an intense period of *individuation,* the process of becoming more uniquely individual.[6] The willfulness demonstrated by adolescents in establishing their independence from parents and, ultimately, from peer groups as well is similar to the tendency of people in the midlife transition to seek to break with some of the conventions and strictures they accepted in the interest of becoming established. Popular images of the man in a midlife crisis who divorces his wife, quits his job, buys a sports car, and takes off for points west is only a caricature of a far more common, subtle, and constructive pattern of reshaping oneself through a new phase of differentiation. As one woman put it, "I used to be afraid of my individuality, feeling like I had to look, dress and act in a certain way. Society does not support uniqueness—there are a lot of pressures to stay in a box and follow the rules."[7]

In *Seasons of a Man's Life*, Levinson and his colleagues point to awareness of one's mortality, as well as some *culminating* event, such as the loss of a close friend or the departure of the youngest child from home, as factors that precipitate self-examination.[8] Culminating events may even be positive; a promotion that represents the achievement of a goal established in early adulthood or a child's college graduation may be equally unsettling in forcing an individual to ask, "Now what?" The goals or dreams that helped shape and motivate the effort to become established are suddenly largely irrelevant.[9]

This *de-illusionment,* as Levinson and his colleagues call it, can indeed lead to a kind of cynical self-absorption and self-indulgence, but often the changes are far more positive. "Getting in touch with oneself" was a celebrated priority of the youthful counterculture of the sixties and seventies, but developmentally it is most generally applicable to midlife. Bernice Neugarten points to the onset of *interiority* at this time, where turning inward in self-examination becomes necessary to deal with the disorientation that comes with an unwillingness to perpetuate the status quo.[10] Much of the focus in this process is on attitudes and behaviors that may no longer be needed to the extent they were in early adulthood. Where the personal skills and resources necessary for child rearing or climbing a corporate ladder are no longer so important, underutilized aspects of oneself become a primary focus. If one has the time, this process of self-examination may take on all the enthusiasm of childhood and adolescent discovery of potential and possibility and, as an attitude toward learning and experience, may last until the end of life. Reestablishing a kind of youthfulness in continued learning and self-discovery enables one to recognize that aging and development are not incompatible.

In *Death of a Hero: Birth of the Soul,* John Robinson makes the case that men achieve their place in society at the expense of more joyous, tender, wondering, and sensuous aspects of the "natural" (magical child) self.[11] He argues that, in spite of centuries of evolution, a hero mythology still directs men into a "compulsive warrior model" where pragmatism and instrumentality require the denial of other characteristics. These characteristics, which hold the "connection to the sacred" in Robinson's view, must be rediscovered in personal expressiveness and sensitivity to the surrounding world.

Traditionally, the pattern for women differs in significant ways. Women are more likely to be focused on caring for and tending to others—to children, husbands, other family members, and friends—rather than being in a struggle against others. But the cost of denying aspects of self in the process is no less significant. And as women increasingly fight the same career battles that men do, often while maintaining home and child care responsibilities, their patterns of self-expression may be even more severely constrained.[12]

Levinson and associates see the work of middle adulthood as a *disengagement* from some of these societal expectations, not to the point of dropping out, but in finding a more personally defined approach to life. Levinson referred to it in 1978 as "becoming one's own man."[13] For Levinson and colleagues, the other-directedness of social accommodation in the individual-society dialectic represents an imbalance that needs redressing, usually in a turn inward and a turn toward self-expression. And while leisure experience is likely to be caught up in patterns of overaccommodation, it is inherently valuable to individuation as well.

Leisure as a Context for Individuation and Self-Renewal

As was noted in Chapter 4, leisure activities often serve to demonstrate a person's membership in a group, to the point that the activity or experience itself may be unimportant. Such affiliation signifies membership both to the individual and to the group. This seems especially important in the years in which one is becoming established; neighborhood picnics, company golf outings and parties, and even frequenting pubs and coffee houses may be crucial in creating and maintaining relationships with people who are already established and potentially influential. *Networking* is a common function of leisure during this period of life.

Establishing a family is similar in some respects. Activities that may be otherwise unappealing are done exclusively "for the children." There are clearly attendant pleasures in watching one's child (and others) in a school play, but parental involvement in children's activities is felt to be a responsibility of the parent role in most cases. This is especially true of mothers, who typically assume more of the burden of child care. One of the participants in a recent study of middle-aged mothers said of her memories of family leisure:

> My mind says that I should say "yes" that I spend leisure time having fun with my children . . . but to me that's not really leisure because I feel like leisure is more self-gratifying, and I wasn't doing anything for myself. I was doing it for my children.[14]

The requirements of early adulthood give way in time to a more leisure-friendly middle age for most people, however, either because children are no longer as demanding, obligatory social events diminish, or one's place in the work context becomes largely secure. Leisure may be appreciated accordingly as a newly found place for reflection, self-expression, and personal enrichment.

Valeria Freysinger's interviews with fifty-four adults between the ages of thirty-six and forty-three revealed that not only did they use leisure regularly to balance role-related stress and boredom, they also used it as a mechanism for creating a sense of personal agency that had been missing in other aspects of their lives.[15] Said a full-time factory worker and mother of two: "In leisure you can become a *person* again. You're not mom, you're not 5,400 on your time card, you're a *person!*" Some of the study participants referred specifically to learning opportunities in leisure. A divorced father of one said, "I love to read. I want to learn to fly. Leisure time I spend *learning* things, OK, the museum and the arts I'm learning now." And others:

> [I spend a lot of my free time] studying how things work and looking at the world like geography, continents, science, architecture, stuff like that, and a lot of that interests me. [divorced father of two; full-time factory worker]

> They [leisure activities] make it possible. They allow me to *be* because I can get away and do leisure activities that enlarge and nurture the other aspects of my *self*. It allows me to get out of myself and learn about other people—it's learning too, as well as refreshing! It changes me and I like it. [divorced mother of one, full-time student][16]

Learning to use leisure to "raise one's existence" in this way may not require a midlife crisis; in fact, it may be the best means of warding off the more dramatic symptoms of the malaise associated with midlife. But for some a period of stagnation precedes a full awareness of life's opportunities and possibilities. As Levinson and his colleagues point out, stagnation may become its own undoing. "Bottoming out" is likely to provoke the kind of interiority that leads one to recognize untapped potentials and to begin the process of becoming what is possible, of finding new sources of self-expression and enjoyment. A renewed interest in doing things and expanding horizons may then be the basis of a pattern of self-discovery that defines the rest of a person's life.

A preoccupation with oneself may, of course, have detrimental effects on relationships and stand squarely in the way of addressing the task of generativity that we will consider shortly; but Levinson and his colleagues also saw cases where a renewed enthusiasm for what life has to offer leads to a posture of some gratitude that is repaid in kindness to others. A person who has plumbed the depths of his or her own circumstances often has special appreciation for the struggles of others. The extent and frequency of such patterns of reciprocity remain to be fully examined, but suffice it to say at this point that self-renewal and social investment are not inherently oppositional. And when they are integrated, it is often in the context of leisure.

Generativity

Erikson presents the issue of *generativity versus stagnation* as the seventh in an eight-stage epigenetic sequence. While Levinson and his colleagues imply that individuation is the predominant task of midlife, Erikson argues that generativity is most likely to preoccupy people in middle adulthood.

> [It is] the concern in establishing and guiding the next generation, although there are individuals who, through misfortune or because of special and genuine gifts in other directions, do not apply this drive to their own offspring. And indeed, the concept generativity is meant to include such more popular synonyms as productivity and creativity, which, however, cannot replace it.[17]

The failure to move toward generativity is reflected in stagnation, which is equated with self-concern, self-indulgence, and personal impoverishment that reflect "the lack of some faith, some 'belief in the species,' which would make a child appear to be a welcome trust of the community."[18] Generativity precedes and sets up the issue of the final stage of life, *ego integrity versus despair*, the question of whether one has a sense of connectedness with and acceptance of all that has come before. Concern with generativity is itself set up, according to Erikson, by connecting intimately with significant others in the preceding period of early adulthood. A union that leads to a preoccupation with raising one or more children may be a source of generativity for either or both partners (though clearly that is not inevitably the case), and caring relationships with others lead to many other ways to contribute to the wider world as well.

The suggestion that generativity can be established in activity that is not directly nurturant of others—in personal productivity and creativity—is somewhat confusing and has led others to see generativity as simply another word for self-actualization.[19] But Erikson asserted that it is the virtue and ethic of *care* that is at issue here, "a widening commitment to *take care of* the persons, the products, and the ideas one has learned *to care for*."[20] Even when one's ideas and products do not have any immediate beneficiary, midlife maturity is reflected in a concern that one's efforts will have some impact on and value for the generations that will follow.

Research on the meaning of generativity has demonstrated the validity of both its prominence at midlife and the dimensionality that Erikson associates with it. Dan McAdams and his colleagues have elaborated on the significance of generativity in the concerns, commitments, actions, and personal narratives of people at midlife in contrast with other periods. Generativity is thus reflected in the processes of creating, maintaining, or providing for those who are to follow. Parenting, teaching, mentoring, counseling, and directing are its prevailing roles. But generating objects and products that are intended to benefit humanity serves the same need.[21]

Concern for impact on future generations, whether in terms of the success of one's children or the endurance of one's inventions and policies, makes generativity a very instrumental purpose. As such it would appear to be antithetical to the more expressive tendencies to be found in leisure. If this is true, what, then, is the role of leisure in generativity?

Leisure as a Context for Generativity

The self-indulgent character of much of leisure activity seems inconsistent with generativity. As noted in Chapter 1, leisure experiences may reflect a variety of "faces," or attitudes and emotions, but they usually include a sense of freedom. The relative freedom from obligation that is the essence of leisure is used primarily for pleasing oneself, even where others are involved.[22] Hedonism may be justified biologically (in sustenance and procreation) and socioeconomically (in perpetuating a market economy); and escapism can be socially adaptive if one is subsequently more responsible and/or effective as a result. Furthermore, enjoyable activity can be both personally adaptive in overcoming negative life events, as I argued in Chapter 6, and important to identity formation, which was the thesis of Chapter 5. But when it comes to contributing to the greater good, leisure is more likely to be regarded as antithetical to generativity, as in the following:

Each individual's middle adulthood is viewed, in these terms, as focusing on a struggle to balance generative expressions (e.g., creativity, procreativity, productivity) with expressions of stagnation (e.g., relaxing, focusing on oneself, taking time out, or, in California, laying back and mellowing out).[23]

Relaxing and focusing on oneself may not lead inevitably to stagnation, but if there is no active investment in the outside world, boredom and self-absorption are likely to follow. If reduced role expectations are not replaced with a repertoire of personally meaningful activities, other mechanisms are used for distraction, diversion, and relaxation from work- or family-related stress. Television watching is the most common solution in such cases, but alcohol and drug use often serve the same purpose. The resignation and cynicism associated with someone who is essentially "done" when the children grow up or the last chance at advancement has passed is caricatured in the man who spends the better part of each weekend in an easy chair drinking beer and watching televised sports. Perhaps for this reason Robert Havighurst identified "establishing meaningful leisure activities" as one of the principal tasks of this period.[24]

Even when leisure is portrayed in terms of its more active variants and its more social contexts, the question of privatism and flight from responsibility comes up. In *Habits of the Heart*, Robert Bellah and his collaborators discuss leisure as one of the primary contexts for individualism and isolationism in contemporary American culture:

With the weakening of the traditional forms of life that gave aesthetic and moral meaning to everyday living, Americans have been improvising alternatives more or less successfully. They engage, sometimes with intense involvement, in a wide variety of arts, sports, and nature appreciation, sometimes as spectators but often as active participants. Some of these activities involve conscious traditions and demanding practices, such as ballet. Others such as walking in the country or jogging may be purely improvisational, though not devoid of some structure or shared meaning. Not infrequently, moments of intense awareness, what are sometimes called "peak experiences," occur in the midst of such activities. At such moments, a profound sense of well-being eclipses the usual utilitarian preoccupations of everyday life. But the capacity of such experiences to provide more than a momentary counterweight to pressures of everyday life is minimal. Where these activities find social expression at all, it is apt to be in the form of what we have called the lifestyle enclave. The groups that form around them are too evanescent, too inherently restricted in membership, and too slight in their hold on their members' loyalty to carry much public weight.[25]

While we may take issue with Bellah with respect to the value of intense private and semiprivate activities for purposes of self-renewal at midlife, we can grant that such experiences contribute little to a sense of generativity. But these critics also fail to recognize that leisure is often the context of service and commitment to others. This fact has not been lost on others who study generativity, however. McAdams and his colleagues measured generativity with a behavior checklist that includes activities likely to be done in the context of leisure such as "taught someone a skill," "read a story to a child," and "attended a neighborhood or community meeting."[26] Such activities can be grouped into three categories: volunteering, mentoring, and youth work.

Volunteerism

Volunteering can take many forms and be associated with a range of experiences, but its primary purpose is to be of service to others.[27] The fact that it is done during one's free time and can be intrinsically enjoyable as well as useful to others makes it a form of leisure as well. But to regard it as exclusively a leisure activity does not sit well with most volunteers. Research indicates that those who volunteer in a wide variety of service activities are not likely to regard their experience as leisure.[28] Whether the volunteer helps others, makes a difference in the quality of community life, or seeks to gain marketable skills and useful contacts, his or her efforts are usually outcome-oriented, worklike, and distinguishable from those generally associated with leisure.

Nevertheless, volunteering at midlife often has a mixture of qualities. In helping to create a good environment for children in the community or providing support services to others, an amiable sociability is usually cultivated around meaning and purpose. Furthermore, such activities are similar to other *serious* forms of leisure activity; indeed, Robert Stebbins includes volunteers as another category of serious leisure along with amateurs and hobbyists.[29] Volunteer firefighters, community association officers, and charity fund raisers, among others, find enjoyment, self-expression, and social identification in their activities, right along with worklike effort, commitment, and perseverance. And in contrast with work per se, volunteers are far less likely to continue in the absence of these intrinsic rewards, whatever the social value of the service.

Those who "work" voluntarily in the context of leisure (organizing interest groups, for example) are not likely to see their activity, however onerous, as volunteering.[30] But a commitment to helping with a voluntary association may provide feelings of generativity comparable to those derived from service work. And as with other leisure activities, the intrinsic interest in the "work" is reflected in the feeling of loss when it can no longer be done for some reason. A participant in the head-injury study referred to in Chapter 6 demonstrated this when she had to give up her various roles of president, fund raiser, registrar, and team captain of a women's soccer organization after a severe automobile accident; she said she missed the organizational roles much more than the soccer itself.

Mentoring

Mentoring appears to be another excellent vehicle for generativity, especially for those without children to nurture or for those whose children have grown up and left home. Mentoring puts a person with more age and experience in a nurturing role with one or more who are younger, but this may include younger adults as well as children. The literature on mentoring, in fact, is almost entirely focused on its use in professional, corporate, and educational contexts, where it has even been institutionalized, with formalized programs in many cases.[31] Mentoring in these contexts contributes to enhanced knowledge, emotional stability, problem solving, decision making, corporate morale, and productivity.[32] This assessment depicts mentoring as almost entirely task oriented, however, which is hardly the role or purpose of leisure. But this corporate version of mentoring has been contrasted with a more natural, expressive, "psychosocial" version that builds relationships outside of and beyond work. And they often work together; the mentoring that goes on in and around the workplace is frequently continued and extended in the context of leisure.[33]

While the focus of the literature on mentoring is usually on adults and career success, there are other mentorlike roles to be found in the context of leisure, where the emphasis is on enjoyment and development in other areas of life. Coaching children in recreational soccer, serving as a big brother or sister, voluntarily teaching a pottery class, or serving as a spiritual mentor on religious matters are examples. Although skill building or expanded understanding may be the objectives of such activities, people usually approach them in a way that maintains a large degree of enjoyment and sociability. When emphasis is put disproportionately on products and outcomes—skills acquired, craftwork produced, victories achieved—intrinsic interest can be undermined. And this is shortsighted in an instrumental sense as well: the generative potential of coaching, teaching, and mentoring often depends, paradoxically, on just the detachment that leisure typically brings, since relaxation and trust create conditions for optimal receptivity and learning readiness. Such situations are generative not only in developing skills but also in cultivating interests that may last a lifetime.

Youth Work

Mentoring with children and adolescents deserves its own category. The best opportunity for finding generativity in leisure is in the nurturance of children, whether they are one's own or others'. The experience of shared enjoyment of activities that are challenging and intrinsically interesting may serve to shape an optimism, a "faith in the future," as Erikson put it, that brings meaning and satisfaction to later life. With one's own children activities can create a bond that is otherwise missing. A bricklayer in Freysinger's study talked about being alienated from his teenage son as a result of working a swing shift that left him with little time when his son was young. With a change in work schedule, he was hoping to engage his son in building a car, noting that "it's such a *growing* time for them, a time that they are picking up on something like that."[34]

In Chapter 4 we considered *transitional* activities, such as music, photography, sports, and games, that combine the best qualities of experience from work and play.[35] The *sponsorship* of adults in these activities is particularly important in making the linkage between childhood and adulthood since their appreciation and support gives the activities credibility and value in the wider world. While the emphasis of this line of research has been on the growing competence of the adolescents for whom the activities were provided, the experience of facilitating that process can reinforce feelings of generativity in the adults involved, while being enjoyable in other respects as well.[36] Using Erikson's framework, Richard Logan points out that the instrumentally oriented *industry* motives of preadolescents are compatible with the instrumentally oriented *generativity* motives of midlife adults, thus creating a kind of symbiotic *cog-wheeling* that makes the coaching relationship very influential for both age groups.[37] Of course, it is important to note that there are probably as many failed relationships between would-be "mentors" and the youth they attempt to influence, especially in adolescence.[38] This is especially true if the adult is *exclusively* outcome oriented.

A Matter of Gender

The business of child care is still characterized by "gender splitting," to use Levinson's term,[39] and leisure is very much a part of that, as has been discussed in previous chapters. The suggestion is that women are more likely to integrate leisure within their role relations[40] and thus, in the context of child rearing anyway, would have a more consistent experience of generativity in leisure. But as was noted in Chapter 2, there is also evidence that because they feel it is their "job," women are *less* likely than men to see the time they spend with children as leisure,[41] that women also find leisure in escape from child care,[42] and that they are likely to see leisure as a context for the resistance of gender-role expectations related to motherhood.[43] It should also be recognized that in taking care of *herself*, a mother provides a positive model of another sort for her children.

As a result of having focused on their careers, men are more likely than women at midlife to feel a deficiency in their responsiveness to others, and to attempt to redress the situation with greater attention to others. Indeed, according to some experts, women are less conscious of generativity in the sense of nurturance at midlife than men and are more oriented to taking action and being outward bound.[44] As men do with respect to nurturance and care giving, women often *cross over* and redress the narrowness that social roles have forced on them by becoming more instrumental in their orientations and expressive patterns.[45]

Reconsidering Generativity and Self-Renewal

It is tempting to suggest, then, that men are more likely to use the freedom of leisure for purposes of generativity, whereas women, for whom caring is often second nature, redress the deficits of their establishment experience in instrumental action and individualistic self-renewal. But this is too limited an understanding of gender differences and of the distinction between generativity and self-renewal as well. Generativity and self-renewal both elicit the dialectic of individual self-expression and social integration, though in different ways. The differentiation and individuation of self-renewal will likely involve others in the course of self-discovery, as companions in the new adventure and as objects of renewed affection and commitment.[46] Similarly, generativity may be reflected in creativity and in the exercise of what Neugarten refers to as the "executive powers" of middle age, where one takes action and uses the power that is available to effect social change.[47] *Agency* is being served in such cases to a greater extent than *communion*;[48] but both factors seem to define generativity in the available research. Using the Thematic Apperception Test in a study of generativity, McAdams and colleagues established that higher levels of generative concerns, actions, and commitments were associated with the sum of power and intimacy motives; they concluded that generativity "implies a blending of agency and communion in human experience."[49] The two factors may exist in varying degrees and may emerge at different times and in different ways in people—as the gender differences identified suggest—but both are reflections of generativity.

Optimizing Leisure for Self-Renewal and Generativity

Self-renewal and generativity in midlife, then, are both indications of positive mental health and developmentally progressive adaptations in the course of aging. The context of leisure affords the freedom for self-expression and social engagement in ways that may not be as available in other contexts, particularly work.

Self-expressive action is thus the most obvious way in which leisure is used to developmental advantage in midlife. But *relaxation* in leisure, where one learns to let go of preoccupying social concerns, may be at least as important at this point in life.[50] Indeed, in the absence of thoughtful consideration and self-examination, action may well prove to be premature and counterproductive with respect to facilitating personal change. The need for relaxation is, of course, well known in contemporary society, as are the prevailing "sedatives" of alcohol and escape into television. But to return to Rollo

May's prescription, those who take full advantage of the *pauses* that life affords for being reflective and receptive to the world around and for cultivating appreciative capacities in an open-minded way are most likely to create conditions supportive of *both* self-renewal and generativity. Of the various faces of leisure, being relaxed in a way that involves openness to experience, reflection, and self-examination may be the most important to living creatively and imaginatively.

Relaxation can have the momentary value of enabling one to adjust effectively to circumstances throughout life, but its existential value is especially important during midlife. Pausing and relaxing thoroughly provides the psychological "distance" necessary to make judgments and effective decisions about what is worth doing next and about how best to use the life that is left to live. These are the questions that are likely to be on the minds of people who are in the fortunate position of being able to make changes in their lives at this point in the life span.

On the other hand, a failure to take action subsequent to such pauses perpetuates disengagement beyond that which is necessary to discover life's possibilities and may reflect continuing stagnation. Taking action is ultimately necessary for self-renewal and generativity. Leisure is valuable for taking action as well as for reflecting on the best action to take. Indeed, the disengagement that occurs in contemplative leisure at midlife is likely to create the conditions for generating the best ideas for the life that will follow.

Conclusion

If we look at the problem of midlife dialectically, it is clear that there is no one solution but rather a need to appreciate the tension between both individual and social needs as a source of growth. A resolution of the tension is likely to involve solutions that are both individually and socially integrative. The bridling at social norms at midlife may begin as a matter of personal rebellion while emerging as an interest in social reform. As Levinson and his colleagues point out, by tempering some of the single-minded achievement orientations of early adulthood, a midlife transition may bring about an enlarged capacity for intimacy and friendship. In this way the "tyranny" of elemental drives and ambitions (and related vanities and animosities) is largely redressed with expansion of such qualities as "wisdom, judiciousness, magnanimity, unsentimental compassion, and breadth of perspective."[51] Leisure may, of course, be associated with the perpetuation of patterns of stagnation and self-indulgence, but it may also be directed to self-renewal, generativity, or both.

The connection of leisure to the contemplative life is a venerable one, harking back to the writings of St. Thomas Aquinas, Plato, and Aristotle.[52] This perspective is consistent with seeing leisure as a product of selective disengagement, relaxation, and private enjoyment. But there are important traditions for the more socially integrative and generative aspects of leisure as well. It is a misrepresentation of classic thought on leisure, according to John Hemingway, to emphasize only its contemplative aspects; the leisure *(schole)* of Plato and Aristotle was the context in which citizens sought to cultivate the civility necessary to exercise the rights of citizenship responsibly and effectively. It was, in Hemingway's words, "a great counter-example to the isolation and fragmentation of modern society."[53]

Josef Pieper suggests that leisure is "the basis of culture" where celebration and affirmation ensure its continuance;[54] and the ritualization of forms of playfulness has been linked to the production of new cultural forms.[55] Clearly the cause of generativity is reflected in these classical notions of leisure, in contrast to more contemporary connotations of leisure. But given the importance of generativity to the social fabric, the power of leisure to engender openness and responsiveness to others in ways that are mutually agreeable may yet come to be recognized as an especially important resource in midlife.

Notes

1. For example, D. Levinson, C. Darrow, F. Klein, M. Levinson, and B. McKee, *The Seasons of a Man's Life* (New York: Alfred Knopf, 1978); A. J. Stewart, C. Franz, and L. Layton, "The Changing Self: Using Personal Documents to Study Lives," *Journal of Personality* 56 (1988): 41–74; S. K. Whitbourne, *The Me I Know: A Study of Adult Identity* (New York: Springer-Verlag, 1986).

2. J. C. Robinson, *Death of a Hero, Birth of the Soul: Answering the Call of Midlife* (Tulsa: Council Oaks Books, 1993); Levinson et al., *The Seasons of a Man's Life;* D. Levinson (with J. Levinson), *Seasons of a Woman's Life* (New York: Alfred Knopf, 1990).

3. B. Neugarten, "Personality and Aging," in J. Birren and K. W. Schaie, eds., *Handbook of the Psychology of Aging* (New York: Van Nostrand Reinhold, 1977).

4. K. Dychtwald and J. Flower, *Age Wave: The Challenges and Opportunities of an Aging America* (Los Angeles: J. P. Tarcher, 1989).

5. See, for example, R. Bellah, R. Madsen, W. Sullivan, A. Swidler, and S. Tipton, *Habits of the Heart* (New York: Harper Row, 1985); C. Lasch, *The Culture of Narcissism* (New York: Norton, 1979).

6. C. Jung, *Man and His Symbols* (New York: Doubleday, 1964).

7. Terri Johnson, one of the women featured in P. Martin, *The Right Side of Forty: Celebrating Timeless Women* (Berkeley, CA: Conari Press, 1997).

8. Levinson et al., *The Seasons of a Man's Life.*

9. With the collaboration of his wife, Judy, Levinson put his findings with men to the test in a sample of forty-five working women (homemakers and corporate and university workers). In *Seasons of a Woman's Life*, Levinson established life change points and patterns in these women that were remarkably consistent with those of the men interviewed in the earlier study. Despite many differences in role-related experiences and continued evidence of what they called "gender splitting" on many issues, the Levinsons became convinced from the data that the theory of adult development established fifteen years earlier with men "held in its broad outline for women as well" (xi).

10. Neugarten, "Personality and Aging."

11. Robinson, *Death of a Hero.*

12. While there are numerous sources for this point, M. C. Bateson's *Composing a Life* (New York: Penguin Books, 1990) is an especially compelling treatment of the subject.

13. Levinson did not identify "becoming one's own woman" as a theme in *Seasons of a Woman's Life*, but he did find in his women respondents similar patterns of individuation in breaking from oppressive conventionality and social expectations in the "structure-changing" phases of middle age.

14. M. D. Bialeschki and S. Michener, "Re-entry to Leisure: Transition Within the Role of Motherhood" (Paper presented at the Canadian Congress on Leisure Research, Winnipeg, Manitoba, 1993).

15. V. J. Freysinger, "The Dialectics of Leisure and Development for Women and Men at Midlife: An Interpretive Study," *Journal of Leisure Research* 27 (1995): 61–84.

16. Ibid., 75.

17. E. Erikson, *Childhood and Society* (New York: Norton, 1963), 267.

18. Ibid.

19. See, for example, K. W. Schaie and J. Geiwitz, *Adult Development and Aging* (Boston: Little Brown, 1982).

20. E. Erikson, *The Life Cycle Completed* (New York: Norton, 1982), 67 (italics in the original).

21. D. McAdams, K. Ruetzel, and J. Foley, "Complexity and Generativity at Midlife: Relations Among Social Motives, Ego Development, and Adults' Plans for the Future," *Journal of Personality and Social Psychology* 50 (1986): 800–807. D. P. McAdams, E. de St. Aubin, and R. L. Logan, "Generativity

Among Young, Midlife, and Older Adults," *Psychology and Aging* 8 (1993): 221–230.

22. For example, S. deGrazia, *Of Time, Work and Leisure* (New York: Anchor, 1962); J. Neulinger, *The Psychology of Leisure* (Springfield, IL: C. C. Thomas, 1981). It is important to note, however, that this view is regarded by some as androcentric, applicable largely to male role structures in Western culture (L. Bella, "Beyond Androcentrism: Women and Leisure," in E. Jackson and T. Burton, eds., *Understanding Leisure and Recreation: Mapping the Past, Charting the Future* [State College, PA: Venture Publishing, 1989]).

23. H. Kivnik, "Interpersonal Relations: Personal Meaning in the Life Cycle," *Contributions to Human Development* 14 (1985): 93–109, 95.

24. R. Havighurst, *Developmental Tasks and Education* (New York: David McKay, 1972). See Table 4.2.

25. Bellah et al., *Habits of the Heart*, 291–292.

26. McAdams, St. Aubin, and Logan, "Generativity Among Young, Midlife, and Older Adults."

27. S. Chambre, *Good Deeds in Old Age* (Lexington, MA: Lexington Books, 1987).

28. P. Hoggett and J. Bishop, "Leisure Beyond the Individual Consumer," *Leisure Studies* 4 (1985): 27–36; S. Parker, "Volunteering as Serious Leisure" (Paper presented at the NRPA Leisure Research Symposium, New Orleans, October 1987).

29. R. Stebbins, *Amateurs, Professionals, and Serious Leisure* (Montreal: McGill-Queen's University Press, 1992).

30. Hoggett and Bishop, "Leisure Beyond the Individual Consumer."

31. S. Barnett, "The Mentor Role: A Task of Generativity," *Journal of Human Behavior* 1 (1984): 15–18; A. Carden, "Mentoring and Adult Career Development: The Evolution of a Theory," *The Counseling Psychologist* 18 (1990): 275–299; S. Merriam, "Mentors and Proteges: A Critical Review of the Literature," *Adult Education Quarterly* 33 (1983): 161–173.

32. Merriam, "Mentors and Proteges."

33. J. Clawson, "Mentoring in Managerial Careers," in C. Derr, ed., *Work, Family, and Career: New Frontiers in Theory and Research* (New York: Praeger, 1980); K. Kram, *Mentoring at Work: Developmental Relationships in Organizational Life* (Glenview, IL: Scott, Foresman, 1985).

34. Freysinger, "The Dialectics of Leisure and Development for Women and Men at Midlife," 72.

35. M. Csikszentmihalyi and R. Larson, *Being Adolescent* (New York: Basic Books, 1984); D. Kleiber, R. Larson, and M. Csikszentmihalyi, "The Experience of Leisure in Adolescence," *Journal of Leisure Research* 18 (1987): 165–176.

36. It is important to see motives of both altruism and mastery in such roles, particularly in coaching children's sports. In discussions of the value of youth sports and the negative effects of excessive emphasis on winning, I am struck by the absence of attention to the intrinsically enjoyable aspects of effectively coaching a team.

37. R. Logan, "A Reconceptualization of Erikson's Theory: The Repetition of Existential and Instrumental Themes," *Human Development* 29 (1986): 128.

38. R. Larson and D. Kleiber, "Free-Time Activities as Factors in Adolescent Adjustment," in P. Tolan and B. Cohler, eds., *Handbook of Clinical Research and Practice with Adolescents* (New York: Wiley, 1992).

39. Levinson, *Seasons of a Woman's Life.*

40. Bella, "Beyond Androcentrism."

41. J. L. Horna, "The Leisure Component of the Parental Role," *Journal of Leisure Research* 21 (1989): 228–241; R. Larson and M. H. Richards, *Divergent Realities: The Emotional Lives of Mothers, Fathers, and Adolescents* (New York: Basic Books, 1994); S. M. Shaw, "Gender Definitions in the Definition and Perception of Household Labor," *Family Relations* 37 (1988): 333–337.

42. Bialeschki and Michener, "Re-entry to Leisure"; K. A. Henderson, "The Meaning of Leisure for Women: An Integrative Review of the Research," *Journal of Leisure Research* 22 (1990): 228–243.

43. B. M. Wearing, "Beyond the Ideology of Motherhood: Leisure as Resistance," *Australian New Zealand Journal of Sociology* 26 (1990): 36–58.

44. D. Gutmann, "The Cross-Cultural Perspective: Notes Toward a Comparative Psychology of Aging," in Birren and Schaie, eds., *Handbook of the Psychology of Aging;* C. Gilligan, *In a Different Voice* (Cambridge, MA: Harvard University Press, 1982.

45. Gutmann, "The Cross-Cultural Perspective." This picture has clearly changed as female career patterns have become more consistent with those of males, but gender differences no doubt still obtain with respect both to generativity and leisure.

46. R. Josselson, "Identity and Relatedness in the Life Cycle," in H. A. Bosma, T. L. Graafsma, H. D. Grotevant, and D. J. de Levita, eds., *Identity and Development* (Thousand Oaks, CA: Sage, 1994).

47. Neugarten, "Personality and Aging."

48. D. Bakan, *The Duality of Human Existence* (Boston: Beacon, 1966).

49. McAdams, Ruetzel, and Foley, "Complexity and Generativity at Midlife."

50. For more on this idea, see D. Kleiber, "Motivational Reorientation in Adulthood and the Resource of Leisure," in D. Kleiber and M. Maehr, eds., *Motivation and Adulthood* (Greenwich, CT: JAI Press, 1985).

51. Levinson et al., *The Seasons of a Man's Life,* 26.

52. deGrazia, *Of Time, Work, and Leisure.*

53. J. Hemingway, "Leisure and Civility: Reflections on a Greek Ideal," *Leisure Sciences* 10 (1988): 179–191.

54. J. Pieper, *Leisure: The Basis of Culture* (New York: Random House, 1963).

55. J. Huizinga, *Homo Ludens* (Boston: Beacon Press, 1955).

8 Engagement, Disengagement, and Integration in Later Life

LINDA LOMAN: It was so nice to see them shaving together, one behind the other, in the bathroom. And going out together. You notice? The whole house smells of
shaving lotion.
WILLY LOMAN: Figure it out. Work a lifetime to pay off
the house. You finally own it and there's nobody to live
in it.
LINDA: Well dear, life is a casting off. It's always that way.
WILLY: No, no, some people—some people accomplish
something.

—Arthur Miller, *Death of a Salesman*

Willy Loman's angst as he nears the end of his working life reminds
us that the issue of generativity continues to be a preoccupation on
into the later years of adulthood.[1] Nevertheless, whether generativity
takes the more benign form of Linda Loman or the more pernicious
form suggested here by Willy, it must submit, like everything else, to
change with age. Gisela Labouvie-Vief pointed out that with advancing age, concern with executive power, competence, and even social
stability often comes to be regarded as a burdensome vestige of the
past, as "the result of a specific social fabric with its pressures toward
restraining the process of individuation." The transition into later life,
she suggested, "brings the most crucial turning point—a chance for
freedom from, and transcendence of, those constraints."[2] Disengag-

ing to some extent from such concerns, without sacrificing connectedness with significant others and the world at large, represents a major challenge for those approaching later life. Certainly one's ongoing social circumstances, personal predispositions, and life history will create differences, but the tension of the individual-society dialectic continues to apply to anyone who is in a position to consider the question, "What's most worth doing at this advanced point in life?"

Having introduced the concept of disengagement in Chapter 7, we turn our attention now to its relevance to later life. However attractive it may be to disengage voluntarily, the change that most clearly defines aging and dying is *involuntary* disengagement, which follows from a confluence of physical changes and social losses. Leisure continues to be the province of volition, however, and making good choices, discriminating even among limited alternatives, will inevitably involve some degree of voluntary disengagement. Margaret and Paul Baltes refer to this process as "selective optimization."[3] Put simply, the voluntary abandonment of some roles and activities affords the freedom to do things of greater interest and for which one has adequate physical, cognitive, and emotional capacity. In this sense disengagement and engagement become partners in the course of adjusting to the opportunities and difficulties of later life; and it is often in leisure that this partnership is worked out.

Adjusting to opportunities and difficulties is a problem with which nearly everyone struggles in later life, to the extent that one has a choice, that is. In such cases disengagement and engagement operate dialectically; they respond to each other. The question of when to go forward and when to pull back are two sides of the same coin. The day that a person withdraws from a civic group, a bridge club, a fitness program, or a volunteer role at the local hospital may also be the day he or she commits to fuller involvement in one of the others. What concerns us here, however, is the impact that such decisions have on development and quality of life. In this chapter we will consider the contributions of engagement and disengagement in making the best of the final period of life, not only in adjusting to the difficulties that arise with aging but also in continuing to develop in spite of those difficulties.

Leisure and Aging Well

What is needed to bring life successfully to completion? There are many ideas about this problem—religious, philosophical, and scientific. From an actuarial perspective, what leads to surviving the *longest* is the important question. But that is not enough for most people. Very few people wish to extend their lives if doing so means living in constant pain and illness. Of course, no one questions the importance of health for those who want simply to endure, and good health certainly can increase the sense of vitality that is a priority to people in later life. But more is usually sought in the interest of finishing one's life story with a satisfying conclusion.

A comfortable standard of living is also a criterion for successful aging. Living in poverty, with basic needs unmet, is a low and unacceptable standard, while the "lifestyles of the rich and famous" represent a standard that exceeds the definition of "comfortable" for most. For those with some wealth and others, too, leisure is a primary source of pleasure as well as a context in which to demonstrate significant material success. Leisure activities signify worldly success, just as they did when Thorsten Veblen wrote his critique of the *leisure class* nearly one hundred years ago. As one contemporary variation has it, "the winner in life is the one who dies with the most toys."

Though wishing for more money and dreaming of winning the lottery is common, people who live simply, with little in the way of material possessions, are usually at least as happy as those who accumulate things. Even those who are disabled or otherwise in poor health manage to have high life satisfaction in many cases. For them, as for most, it is the *meaning* in their lives—the meanings they derive from activities and interactions with significant others and their memories of the past—that contributes the most to their sense of well-being. The creation and re-creation of meaning is also a far more active process than that suggested in the display of possessions. Active involvement, especially with family and close friends who have been a part of one's life, affords a repetition of patterns of self-expression that are personally significant in maintaining and concluding one's life story. On a lake near my home, I encountered an older couple landing their boat after a successful day of bass fishing. I asked if they came to this spot often, and they said, "Not so much in the last few years, but we've been coming here for about thirty years together, and we always bring our grandchildren when they come to visit."

It is clear from a variety of sources that leisure activity is related to a sense of well-being in later life.[4] What remains to be determined is how. The answers are suggested in three theories of successful aging that are typically contrasted. *Activity theory* asserts that people would be happiest and most fulfilled in direct proportion to how much activity they are able to maintain.[5] And indeed there is some evidence that older people who are happier are more active.[6] But the correlations have never been large, and in some cases they are negative.[7] Where there is a positive correlation between the amount of leisure activity and life satisfaction, health is often a confounding variable that is not taken into account. And even when it is controlled, the following question remains: Are people happy because they are active or active because they are happy? Finally, for those experiencing stress and loss, preoccupying activity is often a means of coping, as was discussed in Chapter 6. For example, research on widowhood has indicated that women who have lost their husbands feel a need to "keep busy," and they use leisure activities to that end.[8] But when such patterns represent a degree of denial and interfere with coming to terms with loss or even with the reality of death, they may be maladaptive in the long run.

Another influential albeit largely discredited notion is the *theory of disengagement,* which holds that as the end of life draws near, people voluntarily disengage from others and from their former activity patterns, and society's withdrawal from them in turn leaves them in peace.[9] But the evidence doesn't support the suggestion that people with reduced activities are happier, and the theory drew criticism because it was perceived as legitimizing a pattern of neglect of older people.

The theory that enjoys the most support is *continuity theory,* partly because it is most consistent with other developmental theories of well-being in old age (such as Erik Erikson's) and partly because it has the most empirical support.[10] According to Robert Atchley, continuity is reflected in the fact that "in making adaptive choices, middle-aged and older adults attempt to preserve and maintain existing psychological and social patterns by applying familiar knowledge, skills, and strategies."[11] In continuity theory it isn't the activity per se that is important, it is what the activity and its social context mean to the individual. It stands to reason that those activities and relationships that have been cultivated and maintained over a long period of one's life are the most likely to carry a wealth of meaning and contribute the most to a sense of well-being. The research discussed in Chapter 3, which demonstrates the growing priority of familiar rather than novel activities in later life,[12] provides additional empirical support for continuity theory.

Continuity is threatened in the face of negative life events such as the loss of a spouse or the onset of serious illness, and strong attachment to familiar patterns can make adjusting to such events particularly difficult when lifestyles are dramatically altered as a result. For example, in the case of widows, besides the loss of companionship and social support a spouse may have provided, the social world the couple created is often disrupted as well. But the activities and relationships that do endure in the face of significant life events become all the more important to a person's continuity, stability, and quality of life. A participant in a study of widows reflects on both sides of the continuity issue:

> I've found that after your husband [dies], these friends, they're just . . . gone! They never call, they never come around, you know. . . . I'm talking about the people that you used to . . . go out and eat with, used to go to the lake, be there when they were there, you know. So, when you're alone, most of the things that you do will be done with your children or relatives.[13]

So whether leisure activities are useful in the course of adjusting to changes associated with aging cannot be judged from the frequency or diversity of the activities. Activities must be considered in terms of the experience they bring, their relationship to developmental tasks of later life, social integration, and adaptation to social and physical change. Furthermore, while familiar activities and experiences may gain in importance as the primary source of continuity and meaning in later life, entertaining new leisure possibilities for growth and self-renewal remains important, though perhaps not to the same extent as in midlife. Activities that offer new directions for the development of competence and social integration, like taking painting lessons or serving with the Retired Senior Volunteer Program, for example, have been found to be particularly satisfying.[14] And when such activities come to be regarded as personally expressive and "owned" by the individual, they serve continuity needs as well.

It bears repeating, especially with respect to later life, that we are looking at more than adjustment here. Much has been said elsewhere about how pleasurable activities can distract one from painful and worrisome thoughts; about how doing things with significant others affords the social support necessary to cope with loss; and how being able to participate in activities effectively may be a consolation and source of self-esteem in the face of diminishing capacity in other domains. Such effects are significant and important to any analysis of the value and place of leisure in later life. But, as with earlier ages, leisure is also a context for continuing *development* in later life. Becoming more of what one can be does not end in earlier periods; it is very much involved in later life with this process of seeking and finding meaning. This point was brought home in Helen Lopata's interviews with widows. Signs of personal transformation followed after an initial period of mourning in many cases.[15] Many of these women seemed to find a kind of liberation in the absence of marital responsibilities (especially where the spouse was physically or psychologically abusive or overbearing). And, if financial resources were adequate, they seemed to "bloom" in personal ways. Lopata noted:

> [They] reconstruct their self-concepts, finding support from new social roles and relations, rather than being tied down to people who saw them through a past prism. They report feeling whole and venture into new activities. They travel, join new groups and start new ventures.[16]

As will continue to be demonstrated throughout this chapter, leisure is relevant to the process of growth as well as adjustment in later life.

There are few ideas about growth and adjustment in later life more compelling than Erikson's notion of establishing *ego integrity*. Ego integrity is the feeling of wholeness one reaches in making sense of a life. As was noted in earlier chapters, hierarchical integration is required to reorganize oneself in response to the changes that differentiation brings about; and both of these processes continue until the end of life for most people. But emphasis in later life is on integration, with the difference being that rather than simply adjusting to recent events and changes, the entire life course is the subject of the integration process. Ego integration utilizes leisure through both engagement and disengagement, but actions taken in the context of leisure vary dramatically in their impact on ego integration and on other indicators of progressive adaptation in later life.

Ego Integrity

Ego integrity is the result of having established some internal organization of the self as well as some connection with the rest of the world. Erikson described ego integrity as the acceptance of one's one and only life cycle as something that had to be and that, by necessity, permitted of no substitutions. . . . The possessor of integrity is ready to defend the dignity of his own life style against all physical and economic threats. For he knows that an individual life is the accidental coincidence of but one life cycle with but one segment of history. Ego integrity . . . implies an emotional integration which permits participation by followership as well as acceptance of the responsibility of leadership.[17]

Consistent with his progressive model of development, Erikson asserted that generativity is a precondition of ego integrity; a sense of being part of the world, of having contributed to it in some way, enables one to conclude a life story in a meaningful and acceptable way. Most people, regardless of their economic resources, are concerned with their "legacy." To avoid the *despair* that is the antithesis of ego integrity, it is not enough to find meaning in only a personal, self-reflective process; connections to others—whether family, neighborhood, or nation—are also at issue. Although one's personal future may be limited, a concern for leaving the world as well off as possible prompts interest in the problems that younger generations are and will be facing. Nevertheless, some amount of despair may be inevitable.

Erikson and his colleagues came to a better understanding of later life despair after interviewing a group of people between the ages of seventy and ninety.[18] In these interviews the investigators found considerably more evidence of despair than they expected—over regrettable aspects of the past that can't be changed, over aspects of the present that are painful, and over a future that is uncertain for one's offspring and frightening in the prospects of inescapable death and perhaps suffering—even among otherwise enthusiastic and well-integrated individuals. Erikson and his colleagues concluded that some despair must be acknowledged and managed in a balanced way that also allows the work of integration.

Despair over the past is best dispelled through self-acceptance. One's impact on others must come to be understood in relation to limitations as well as abilities, with a certain amount of forgiveness granted oneself for past failings or transgressions, but typically, the past is remembered selectively and what is remembered is recast in a more favorable light to allow the future to be lived continuously and positively.[19] In any case, some amount of life review is necessary for ego integration; avoiding coming to terms with the past makes despair more extreme.

Life review and reminiscence are necessary to do the work of accepting oneself and one's place in family and/or cultural history.[20] Understanding and accepting oneself is an important part of the process. Reminiscence can be done alone—as in a kind of life review—or casually with others, but in either case it reinforces continuity and helps contribute to a sense of integrity. When it is done socially—whether sharing stories with grandchildren, as part of a program in a long-term care facility, or in some other context—it provides an opportunity to use feedback to validate and construct a coherent narrative. Rather than remembering one's life as just "one damned thing after another," such interchanges allow for the interpretation of all experiences, regrettable or not, as integral parts of one's life story.

Even in swapping tales while waiting for a bus with a neighbor, the re-creation of past experience benefits ego integration. Recalling the distant past may, in fact, be easier than remembering events of a week earlier; cognitive deficits that may accompany aging are less likely to impair remote memories that are the subject of reminiscence than they are short-term memory processes. Furthermore, there is some evidence that the activity of reminiscence itself has the effect of maintaining a degree of cognitive plasticity and social connectedness.[21] The adage "use it or lose it" applies here, even if "it" is merely the mental process of reliving the old days.

Is this preoccupation with days gone by enough, though, to capture the best that life has to offer in its later stages? One imagines a rather stodgy old man recounting past adventures and adversities in serious but pleasant conversation with a companion. If this image is unappealing, perhaps it is because it can be contrasted with culturally shaped idealizations of youthful vitality that ignore the realities of aging and dying. Clearly, the relative physical passivity of later life may belie what is an active mental process associated with both social and private reminiscence.

Nevertheless, we need only look to the aging themselves to see an endless variety of outward-bound, present-centered patterns of activity. If Erikson is right, the integration function will hold sway in the end, but to see ego integration as only a matter of reflection would be a mistake. Meaning is to be found in action as well.

Engagement

By engagement I mean the initiation of action to perpetuate current interests and relationships or establish new ones. It is purposeful involvement in the world, intended to re-create meaning and maintain continuity or create new possibilities for oneself and others. Continuing to serve on the board of a local hospital auxiliary is an example of continuing engagement, while taking the initiative to recruit a speaker for the association's next meeting might reflect an interest in change. Experimentalism in later life is considerably less likely among those who are frail and vulnerable, but age itself does not bring an end to the process of differentiation. Indeed, seeing oneself as a learner and as a cultivator of new experience may be an essential self-definition to be integrated into the course of a life review. Joan and Erik Erikson, with Helen Kivnik, discuss a wide variety of "vital involvements," including work-related activities (e.g., remodeling, gardening, financial manipulations), grandparenting, lifelong learning, and the arts. With respect to the arts they note that older people have more time for sensory immersion than middle-aged people typically have; and they are inclined to do their utmost to "alert and empower the aging body to remain actively involved."[22]

Engagement is also likely to produce a variety of discrete experiences, from the intense, flowlike experience of committed, effortful application of abilities such as preparing a special dish to the more casual, open-focused attention of listening to a poetry reading. Television watching may be very stimulating and involving, but the effort required is limited and thus is unlikely to generate any sense of control or competence. Knitting an afghan, gardening, or playing the piano can bring about the same intense, flow-producing involvement that is associated with high investment activity in earlier periods.

Still another kind of engagement is that of simply tending to the "daily round" of chores. While it might seem misleading to suggest that these are leisure activities, they become enjoyable when done in a leisurely way. Watering the plants and tending to pets are often described as activities that are more a matter of leisure than work; and as routines they can be a source of continuity and stability. They provide a "rhythm of comfortable predictability."[23] In the Erikson study referred to earlier, the experience was illustrated by the women who said, "I can't wait to get into bed at night with a good book. And I can't wait to get up in the morning and have a cup of coffee."[24] As with other kinds of engagement, even daily routines can be mood elevating and distracting from other sources of anxiety, stress, loneliness, and depression. Involvement that requires more intensity, however, is likely to be more useful developmentally.

The ideas of flow and high-investment leisure were discussed thoroughly in earlier chapters, but these experiences are common to later life as well. What is important to consider with respect to later life, however, is the deeper *meaning* in the activity. To be able to express one's competence is clearly a source of continuing self-esteem, but the connection to ego integration may be less obvious. While involvement with novel, flow-producing activities can be differentiating and growth-producing, intense involvement in familiar activities that reinforce enduring aspects of the self are generally more appealing. Activities that have a "career" quality are an important source of what Atchley refers to as *inner continuity*, the psychological property that people seek in later life as an underpinning to ego integrity.[25] Familiar activities remain flow-producing and challenging because their inherent challenges continue to be elaborated and because a person has the ability to manipulate the activities to make them more challenging. Furthermore, the *external continuity* that is often provided with such activities—the same places, companions, and conditions—contributes to a sense of social integration as well. For example, an aging collector of antique lamps would not only continue to attend local auctions but might also subscribe to trade magazines that locate lamps in existence around the country and interact via the Internet with others who share the interest.

Roger Mannell identified candidates for "good" leisure in later life in his review of Jack Kelly's work on high-investment activities, Stebbins's work on serious leisure, and Csikszentmihalyi's work on flow. These concepts apply similarly to activities that "have been developed over time, require a great deal of effort and resources, require the acquisition of skill, and are most likely to yield an enhanced sense of competence and worth."[26] What they lack in spontaneity and variety they make up for in commitment and intensity, while still having enough freedom and enjoyment to be regarded as leisure. Included are a wide variety of things such as gardening, tinkering around the house, and playing with grandchildren, anything in which one could become repeatedly absorbed.

Mannell and colleagues asked a sample of ninety-two retired older adults to wear pagers and keep journals in which they reported their experiences when they were (randomly) beeped.[27] The researchers found higher affect and other indicators of flow when people were involved in high-investment activities; but contrary to expectations, flow seemed to be facilitated when there were some *extrinsically* reinforcing conditions such as those associated with a sense of obligation. They concluded that without commitment, even with freedom to choose, flow-type experience was less common. Most important, the percentage of time in flow activities significantly predicted life satisfaction for these older adults.

Some of the explanation for the unexpected finding related to motives for activity involvement in this study may lie in the characteristics of the age group studied. As we noted in Chapter 2, history must be recognized as a determinant of developmental change. Persons who grew up during the Depression of the 1930s, for example, have been shown to place less value on leisure than those of other cohorts.[28] They are, as a result, more likely to demonstrate a "busy ethic" that "legitimates the leisure of retirement . . . defends retired people against judgments of senescence, and . . . gives definition to the retirement role."[29] In other words, leisure is all right for this cohort group only if it is used "productively."

The fact that the participants in Mannell's investigation were likely to identify instrumental payoffs when justifying their involvement in high-investment activities is due in part to the value systems of their age cohort. This age group, most of whom were children during the Depression, are especially likely to get involved in those activities that they believe have some redeeming social value and somewhat less likely to invest much time in activities for their own sake. But to say that they were extrinsically motivated is to miss the intrinsic satisfaction they apparently derived from what they were doing, whatever its extrinsic payoffs. More to the point is that the identity of this age group is tied to working hard and being productive. Indeed, this is part of the meaning for them and contributes to their sense of identity and integrity.

Perhaps subsequent cohorts are or will be less attached to the productive significance of their activities; but the value of the activities in which they engage will be no less tied to their meaning systems. As Waterman has pointed out about personal expressiveness, one's personal characteristics and central purposes in life come together in defining the meaning of activities.[30] And continuing involvement in those activities that require the special talents and interests of an individual, because they are self-defining and socially significant, are likely to bring enduring meaning in later years.

Such activity-specific benefits notwithstanding, the greatest impact of activity involvement comes in doing the activities with others. By providing the *connectedness* so important to ego integrity, the activity itself may be largely irrelevant at times. In fact, research on activity involvement as a contributor to well-being in later life often fails to account for the effects of social context and the associated relationships, whether they be friendships or family.[31] Actions engaged in together can be important for the relationship, even if the activity has little personal significance: the casual structure of many leisure activities often provides the ideal context for self-disclosure, resource exchange, and displays of affection, thus solidifying the relationship.[32] In this sense, shared involvement in *any* activity may contribute to feelings of connectedness and ego integrity.

The best of both worlds may come in sharing activities that are particularly meaningful to both or all participants. Shared enjoyment may contribute as much to meaningful integration in later life as it does to intimacy in earlier adulthood. While it may be true that suffering and struggling is a bonding experience, much of the pleasure of romantic love is sought and found in shared activity and especially, as was noted earlier, in *shared flow*.[33] The intense enjoyment that is felt when skills and challenges are effectively matched in an activity seems to be magnified if that happens in interaction with another.

Finally, participation in organized group activities such as political action groups, service organizations, or churches is also important to the quality of later life. Certainly attachment to the community is reinforced by such activities. Volunteer work can also be a source of feelings of generativity, which in turn provide a basis for ego integration, as noted earlier. More than two-thirds of people over sixty-five belong to voluntary organizations in the United States, and nearly as many go to church once per month or more.[34] The impact of such activities is not entirely clear; however, the accumulated evidence suggests that only church-going has a positive impact on adjustment (and church goers are not inclined to look at this activity as leisure).[35] The impact of voluntary activities on ego integrity and other indicators of well-being remains to be fully determined. And there may even be a disadvantage to ego integrity in being overly involved in a wide variety of activities. In such cases disengagement may be the healthiest alternative. Though we previously touched on disengagement theory and its association with ageist beliefs, disengagement in leisure can enable one to refocus time, energy, and physical capacities in activities that provide the greatest source of personal satisfaction.

Disengagement

In many social programs for the elderly, keeping active is almost a mantra. "Use it or lose it" applies to both mental and physical abilities. Engagement is clearly seen as the healthiest alternative in later life, even if only as a distraction in coping with necessary losses. To believe otherwise is assumed to be a sign of resignation. But social scientists have not always sung the praises of an active, outward-bound lifestyle in later life. As noted in the discussion of theories of successful aging, there was a time when disengagement was assumed to be the healthiest posture to have in later life.

Disengagement was introduced in the last chapter to capture both role disengagement—what Levinson and his colleagues referred to as "detribalization," the relinquishing of unnecessary and unwanted social entanglements—and the action taken to create leisure more subjectively. While disengagement in the sociological sense means the relinquishing of social roles in a relatively permanent and public manner, we may also look at it psychologically as the experience of separating from some patterned involvement and relaxing.[36] Both kinds of disengagement can have a liberating effect, even when not truly chosen, such as with retirement from oppressive working conditions or with the death of an overbearing spouse. The resulting freedom can bring about a luxurious peacefulness or serve as the basis for dynamic self-transforming engagements. But disengagement as a pattern is often alarming when it seems to be an indication of resignation from life, a prelude to dying.

As noted earlier, disengagement has a controversial intellectual past.[37] The theory asserted that disengagement may be initiated by either the individual or society but that it will eventually be the option of choice for both and that the individual will fare better as a result. The research that followed the development of this theory did not offer a great deal of support; people continued to prefer to be actively engaged, and those who would seek to sever ties with older people as a function of age were regarded as ageist.[38] People experience disengagement in a total sense not as a matter of preference but only as a result of disabling physical conditions or the loss of resources. Continuity theory has replaced disengagement as a better explanation for what people seek in later life.

Nevertheless, one of the more salvageable tenants of the original disengagement theory is that a "reduction in the number and variety of interactions leads to an increased freedom from the control of the norms governing everyday behavior."[39] This "increased freedom" needs to be recognized as a positive outcome if it is the result of a person's preferences. *Selective* disengagement from some circumstances may actually facilitate attention to those matters that are most crucial and engagement in those activities that are most important.[40]

Reducing peripheral social relationships can also be important to preserving emotional well-being.[41] There is some evidence that unwanted social interaction has a more deflating effect on well-being than positive interaction has an enhancing effect.[42] And even when interaction occurs with supportive and trusted others, there are times when it is unwelcome, especially when offers of help bring up stressful associations. Loneliness is a common problem in later life, especially for those who have no choice in the matter, but solitude is quite often a preferred condition.

Among the ninety-two retired Canadians referred to, being alone was associated with low levels of affect and arousal for those who lived by themselves, but for those living with spouses, time alone was actually associated with a more optimal level of arousal, concentration, and sense of challenge.[43] Apparently, time alone—almost 40 percent of the free time available to the married people sampled—was used as an opportunity to engage in other things. And rather than being a reflection of antisocial patterns, the kinds of activities engaged in alone often had implications for others, such as in making things for one's children. The disengagement in this case is only a prelude to another kind of engagement.

When it is voluntary, the act of disengagement often has the effect of establishing the context of leisure, however it is subsequently used.[44] Stepping back psychologically frames the situation as more clearly one's own, to be used for personal advantage, whatever that may be. The developmental advantage of disengagement, at least when it is a matter of choice, is that it can bring about the kind of control that is necessary for both self-assessment and self-expression. Reminiscence and life review become more likely when one is not staying busy and actively involved. Reverie for solitary reminiscence or discussion of past events with intimate friends or family members requires time and some freedom from expectations.

Disengagement serves some people better than others. To be able to be truly relaxed and peaceful may take emotional stability to begin with. In the early Kansas City studies of subjective well-being in later life, investigators identified several "types" who were most satisfied with life.[45] These included a group who had fulfilling patterns of engaging activity but also a group who seemed able to be happy and satisfied with a limited pattern of activities and a relatively passive lifestyle. The investigators called this group the "rocking-chair" type and contrasted them with another group, the "armored-defensive," who were neurotically active and unable, apparently, to relax. While there are clearly individual differences in the patterns of activity that are most adaptive and satisfying in later life, vigorous activity is not necessarily an indicator of positive mental health; nor is the lack of overt activity an indicator of the absence of well-being.

Disengaging selectively also allows more energy for those activities that are more personally important. Selective disengagement thus enables continuity of activity and interests that are most meaningful and personally integrative. Discriminating among alternative action possibilities may mean the abandonment of some roles and relationships, but the benefit to other activities and relationships will usually justify the changes.[46] The creation of time and the selection of more meaningful patterns and relationships are also likely to contribute to ego integration.

Integration

> *I told my son: triage*
> *is the main art of aging.*
> *At midlife, everything*
> *sings of it. In law*
> *or healing, learning or play,*
> *buying or selling—above all*
> *in remembering—the rule is*
> cut losses, let profits run.
> *Species rise and fall*
> *by selection, which is triage;*
> *even the beautiful,*

> *gleaming as if timeless—*
> *a standing wave in the flood*
> *that washes all away—*
> *is a species of survival.*
> —From "Triage: An Essay"[47]

The problem of later life, at least for people who have the life circumstances to be concerned with more than just survival, is essentially a triage in three parts: (1) how to disengage from those activities that are no longer fulfilling; (2) how to stay engaged with those activities that have provided a worthwhile return on investments of time and energy; and (3) how to become engaged in patterns that may only now present themselves as attractive alternatives. The challenges implied in this agenda are considerable. Disengaging effectively—deciding what to let go, how to let it go, and when—may be a question of competence in some cases, but since others are usually involved, it will rarely be done without a thought. Saying good-bye to activities and involvements may be as difficult as saying good-bye to close friends. In fact, they may be one and the same at times.

Disengagement is often necessary in addressing the challenges of aging, but it is seldom sufficient. The freedom that disengagement provides may be vacuous and distressing if one is not prepared to optimize other areas, explore new directions, or rediscover old ones. Nor is psychological readiness always enough. Even if one has the advantage of financial resources and sufficiently good health to afford continued engagement, other forces act to constrain activity, not the least of which is that society still expects very little of older people in general.[48] Fortunately, as was noted earlier, concern with social opinion also dissipates with age.

Meaningfulness is critical to the triage process. Finding some coherence with the past and future is nearly always going to be important to the quality of one's later life. For a person with an identity that includes learner and risk taker, new and unfamiliar opportunities may be welcomed; but without such an orientation, changing circumstances are likely to be disorienting and even disintegrative. Selection of opportunities for investing attention and energy is a highly personal matter of considerable complexity. In any case, disengagement and engagement cannot be considered in isolation; they are both necessary to the purpose of achieving ego integration in later life. The transition of retirement provides a useful focus for further clarifying these processes.

Retirement

Even when it is voluntary, disengagement from the roles of work is difficult. The loss of status, patterned activity, and predictable association, while not generally as painful as the experience of unexpected unemployment in earlier periods of adulthood, nonetheless creates a void that requires considerable psychic attention.[49] But the transition itself can lead to a kind of reorganization of the self and social identity, allowing competence and vitality to be reconstructed in more personal ways.

In an interview study of thirty-two recently retired men and women, Mark Luborsky found that most of the participants turned to their homes and the surrounding outdoor space in reorganizing their lives.[50] They spoke enthusiastically about having the time to engage in special projects related to housecleaning and landscaping/gardening. The critical factor, though, was laboring *alone*; his respondents showed patterns of retreat from the public eye, working on the interior of the house or the backyard before moving out to the front yard and back into the community. Luborsky identified the following stages: (1) secluding the self; (2) denuding and loosening ties to the earth and the social estate; (3) recontouring space for renewed productivity; (4) redefining cultural ideals for independence; and (5) using projects as starting points to reorganize social lives. And despite retiring from white-collar as well as blue-collar jobs, nearly all sought a connection with physical labor, "getting right down to the dirt of the matter."

Luborsky considered alternative explanations for the attraction to such activities (such as *flow*, taking a break, or just staying busy), but none accounted for the timing and sequencing of experiences, the emphasis in the early stages on privacy, and the focus on the physical. The projects themselves he regarded as providing "a thorough leveling of social and personal landscapes" for the purpose of reestablishing oneself, in the face of cultural messages to the contrary, as retaining the competence to be a "working adult."[51] In some cases the work provided autonomy, self-sufficiency, and evidence of the strength that was missing in the jobs from which they had retired. The home environment, in his view, provided new spaces and new meanings in addressing developmental tasks, particularly the generativity that is served in working on something that would endure for others to follow.

This focus on physical labor and home maintenance gave way to other interests as the retirement transition progressed for Luborsky's respondents. He interpreted the progression as a kind of recapitulation of the life span: playing in the yard to recapture childhood; "spousing" to recreate and restore intimacy to relationships; and housecleaning, which allowed life review through attention to valued objects. Most of the respondents in Luborsky's study were also involved in volunteerism and community service, and they looked on the first phases of their retirement process in retrospect as rather "selfish," perhaps not appreciating the full significance of the process.

The limited sample in this study (all Caucasian and middle to upper middle class) suggests caution in generalizing; having a house and property to attend to certainly facilitates the transformation reported here. But the point to be taken from the study is that both disengagement and engagement were implicated in the reorganization of self that occurred in this transition where the past was reconstructed in a way that facilitated personal integration.

Leisure interests and activities may be as important to personal integration in later life as they are to identity formation in earlier years. In fact, these two markers of development are affected similarly by activity. While the exploration of interests is revealing of individual potential, some continuity of interest is necessary both to solidify identity and preserve integrity. And yet it is important to recognize that growth motives last throughout life and that a departure from regular patterns of activity is not inevitably disintegrative. As noted earlier, one's identity as a learner and as a creative interpreter of life can be reconciled with declining capacities in the integration process. Strict adherence to the old and familiar is a reflection of rigidity; flexibility may be the most valuable ingredient in adjusting to later life losses.[52] Abandoning the old and considering the new is adaptive right to the end of life.

Conclusion

Value judgments can be the nemesis of scientific investigation, but on the subject of aging in later life, they abound. Maybe what is wanted and needed in later life is clearer than in earlier periods. For middle- and upper-class individuals with the resources to arrange it, self-indulgence is often the simple priority, with little more than the assertion that it is their right. "I've earned it" or "I'm entitled," a person might say. A social payback is in order for having served one's country in one way or another or having successfully brought up children. And defending that prerogative may be the most compelling part of growing old for some. Integrity may be first and foremost a physical and spatial priority: protecting one's being, one's personal property, and one's niche in life. People who have suffered illness or serious insult to their bodies and find their physical integrity at risk have few resources to look for anything more. But often such people are the first to recognize that there is more to life than just feeling well and having things.

The idea of aging clearly suffers from a bad image, at least in Western culture. Perhaps, as has been argued, industrialization has stripped age of its status as a font of wisdom and tradition.[53] Whereas we recognize the refinement that aging brings to wines, we seem far less likely to acknowledge similar patterns with human beings. Maybe this follows from our view that aging takes people, albeit against their will, "into that dark night." The inevitability of death tends to make us see aging only as decline. And if development unfolds according to some genetically coded set of instructions, the lack of control seems even more depressing.

But this chapter was not about adjusting to aging and dying. While there is compelling evidence that leisure experience is important in coping with the loss and limitation that aging brings, we have dealt here, as in earlier chapters, with its role in development, a process that can continue right to the end of life. And as in earlier periods, development in the course of aging benefits from both engagement and disengagement.

Engagement and disengagement are actions that apply to both role relationships and psychological processes. In later life, the relaxation of disengagement is important in managing the stress associated with the loss of personal and social resources but also in creating the context for life review and reminiscence that are so important to ego integration. Intense, high-investment engagement, on the other hand, may be similarly generative of a sense of integrity, albeit in a more active way. Life can continue to be vibrant as well as meaningful. Indeed, meaningful self-expression, enjoyable interaction, and peaceful repose enrich the final chapters of one's life story in ways that may be reminiscent of the best of the past.

Notes

1. See, for example, D. P. McAdams, E. de St. Aubin, and R. L. Logan, "Generativity Among Young, Midlife, and Older Adults," *Psychology and Aging* 8 (1993): 221–230.

2. G. Labouvie-Vief, "Proactive and Reactive Aspects of Constructivism: Growth and Aging in Life-Span Perspective," in R. Lerner and N. Busch-Rossnagel, eds., *Individuals as Producers of Their Own Development* (New York: Academic Press, 1981), 218. Labouvie-Vief's view suggests further that if generativity takes precedence at midlife in the Eriksonian sense, the need for disengagement and individuation identified by Levinson may only be delayed as a result.

3. P. Baltes and M. Baltes, "Psychological Perspectives on Successful Aging: The Model of Selective Optimization with Compensation," in P. Baltes and M. Baltes, eds., *Successful Aging: Perspectives from the Behavioral Sciences* (Cambridge: Cambridge University Press, 1990).

4. For example, C. Riddick, "Life Satisfaction of Older Males and Females," *Leisure Sciences* 7 (1985): 47–64; R. Russell, "The Importance of Recreation Satisfaction and Activity Participation to the Life Satisfaction of Age-Segregated Retirees," *Journal of Leisure Research* 19 (1987): 273–283.

5. N. Hooyman and H. Kiyak, *Social Gerontology*, 4th ed. (Boston: Allyn Bacon, 1996).

6. See R. O. Ray and G. Heppe, "Older Adult Happiness: The Contributions of Activity Breadth and Intensity," *Physical and Occupational Therapy in Geriatrics* 4 (1986): 31–43, for a review of some of this evidence.

7. Ibid.

8. C. D. Harvey and H. M. Bahr, *The Sunshine Widows: Adapting to Sudden Bereavement* (Lexington, MA: Lexington Books, 1980); I. Patterson and G. Carpenter, "Participation in Leisure Activities After the Death of a Spouse," *Leisure Sciences* 16 (1994): 105–117; A. Sharp and R. C. Mannell, "Participation in Leisure as a Coping Strategy Among Bereaved Women," *Proceedings of the Eighth Canadian Congress on Leisure Research* (Ottawa: University of Ottawa, 1996).

9. E. Cumming and W. Henry, *Growing Old* (New York: Basic Books, 1961).

10. R. Atchley, "A Continuity Theory of Normal Aging," *The Gerontologist* 29 (1988): 183–190; R. C. Atchley, "Continuity Theory and the Evolution of Activity in Later Adulthood," in J. R. Kelly, ed., *Activity and Aging: Staying Involved in Later Life* (Newbury Park, CA: Sage, 1993).

11. Atchley, "Continuity Theory and the Evolution of Activity in Later Adulthood," 5.

12. S. E. Iso-Ahola, E. Jackson, and E. Dunn, "Starting, Ceasing, and Replacing Leisure Activities over the Lifespan," *Journal of Leisure Research* 26 (1994): 227–249.

13. B. Wilhite, K. Sheldon, and N. Jekubovich-Fenton, "Leisure in Daily Life: Older Widows Living Alone," *Journal of Park and Recreation Administration* 12 (1994): 64–78.

14. J. R. Kelly, M. Steinkamp, and J. Kelly, "Later-Life Satisfaction: Does Leisure Contribute?" *Leisure Sciences* 9 (1987): 189–200; R. Mannell, "High-investment Activity and Life Satisfaction Among Older Adults: Committed, Serious Leisure, and Flow," in J. R. Kelly, ed., *Activity and Aging: Staying Involved in Later Life* (Newbury Park, CA: Sage, 1993).

15. H. Z. Lopata, *Women as Widows: Support Systems* (Durham, NC: Duke University Press, 1979); "Widows: Social Integration and Activity," in J. R. Kelly, ed., *Activity and Aging* (Newbury Park, CA: Sage, 1993).

16. Lopata, "Widows," 103.

17. E. H. Erikson, *Childhood and Society* (New York: Norton, 1963), 268–269.

18. E. H Erikson, J. M. Erikson, and H. Q. Kivnick, *Vital Involvement in Old Age* (New York: W. W. Norton, 1986).

19. See, for example, M. A. Lieberman and S. S. Tobin, *The Experience of Old Age: Stress, Coping, and Survival* (New York: Basic Books, 1983).

20. R. N. Butler, "The Life Review: An Interpretation of Reminiscence in the Aged," in B. L. Neugarten, ed., *Middle Age and Aging: A Reader in Social Psychology* (Chicago: University of Chicago Press, 1968); R. G. Parker, "Reminiscence: A Continuity Theory Framework," *The Gerontologist* 35 (1995): 515–525.

21. Parker, "Reminiscence."

22. Erikson, Erikson, and Kivnik, *Vital Involvement in Old Age*, 319.

23. Atchley, "Continuity Theory of Normal Aging." See also A. Della Fave and F. Massimini, "Modernization and the Changing Contexts of Flow in Work and Leisure," in M. Csikszentmihalyi and I. Csikszentmihalyi, eds., *Optimal Experience: Psychological Studies of Flow in Consciousness* (New York: Cambridge University Press, 1988), for a study of older shepherds in the Italian Alps who have managed to preserve a flowlike quality in daily work and subsequent generations in the region who have not.

24. Erikson, Erikson, and Kivnik, *Vital Involvement in Old Age*, 62.

25. Atchley, "Continuity Theory and the Evolution of Activity in Later Adulthood."

26. Mannell, "High-Investment Activity and Life Satisfaction Among Older Adults," 127; Kelly, Steinkamp, and Kelly, "Later-Life Satisfaction," 194.

27. R. Mannell, J. Zuzanek, and R. Larson, "Leisure States and the Flow Experience: Testing Perceived Freedom and Intrinsic Motivation Hypotheses," *Journal of Leisure Research* 20 (1988): 289–304.

28. G. Elder, *Children of the Great Depression* (Chicago: University of Chicago Press, 1974).

29. D. J. Ekerdt, "The Busy Ethic: Moral Continuity Between Work and Retirement," *The Gerontologist* 26 (1986): 239–244.

30. A. S. Waterman, "Personal Expressiveness: Philosophical and Psychological Foundations," *Journal of Mind and Behavior* 11 (1990): 47–74.

31. R. G. Adams, "Activity as Structure and Process: Friendships in Older Adults," in J. R. Kelly, ed., *Activity and Aging: Staying Involved in Later Life* (Newbury Park, CA: Sage, 1993).

32. Ibid.

33. M. Csikszentmihalyi, "Love and the Dynamics of Personal Growth," in K. S. Pope, ed., *On Love and Loving* (San Francisco: Jossey-Bass, 1980).

34. S. J. Cutler and N. L. Danigelis, "Organized Contexts of Activity," in J. R. Kelly, ed., *Activity and Aging: Staying Involved in Later Life* (Newbury Park, CA: Sage, 1993).

35. Ibid.

36. D. Kleiber, "Motivational Reorientation in Adulthood and the Resource of Leisure," in D. Kleiber and M. Maehr, eds., *Motivation and Adulthood* (Greenwich, CT: JAI Press, 1985).

37. W. A. Achenbaum and V. L. Bengtson, "Re-engaging the Disengagement Theory of Aging: On the History and Assessment of Theory Development in Gerontology," *The Gerontologist* 34 (1994): 756–763.

38. Ibid.

39. Cumming and Henry, *Growing Old*, 213.

40. While Paul and Margaret Baltes ("Psychological Perspectives on Successful Aging") don't use the word "disengagement," this is an essential part of the selection function of "selective optimization."

41. L. L. Carstenson, "Motivation for Social Contact Across the Lifespan: A Theory of Socioemotional Selectivity," *Nebraska Symposium on Motivation* (Lincoln: University of Nebraska Press, 1993).

42. K. S. Rook, "The Negative Side of Social Interaction: Impact on Psychological Well-Being," *Journal of Personality and Social Psychology* 46 (1984): 1097–1108.

43. R. Larson, J. Zuzanek, and R. Mannell, "Being Alone Versus Being with People: Disengagement in the Daily Experience of Older Adults," *Journal of Gerontology* 40 (1985): 375–381.

44. See Kleiber, "Motivational Reorientation in Adulthood," for more on this view of leisure.

45. R. J. Havighurst, B. L. Neugarten, and S. S. Tobin, "Disengagement and Patterns of Aging," in B. Neugarten, ed., *Middle Age and Aging* (Chicago: University of Chicago Press, 1968).

46. Baltes and Baltes, "Psychological Perspectives on Successful Aging."

47. P. Hamill, "Triage: An Essay," *The Georgia Review* 45 (1991): 463–469.

48. F. McGuire, "Constraints in Later Life," in M. G. Wade, ed., *Constraints on Leisure* (Springfield, IL: C. C. Thomas, 1985).

49. Gender differences should be noted here. While dramatic changes in the employment status of women in the past several decades suggest that the gap is narrowing, men are still far more likely to have left jobs with the ritualized transition of retirement and with related institutionalized preparation for it. And even with comparable work lives outside the home, retirement is still less likely to provide the freedom that it does for men, since women still assume more of the domestic burden in most cases.

50. M. R. Luborsky, "The Retirement Process: Making the Process and Cultural Meanings Malleable," *Medical Anthropology Quarterly* 8 (1994): 411–429.

51. Ibid., 414.

52. Baltes and Baltes, "Psychological Perspectives on Successful Aging."

53. B. McPherson, *Aging as a Social Process* (Toronto: Butterworth, 1990).

Index